Ethnic Chinese Entrepreneurship in Malaysia

The study of ethnic Chinese in Southeast Asia has a long tradition. What is most striking in these studies is just how difficult it is to generalise about this ethnic group in the region. Whether or not they have been able to identify as Chinese has to a certain extent depended on different processes of social and political engineering, which in turn make them more or less distinct as an ethnic group. In the case of Malaysia, national political schemes such as the affirmative action policy indirectly force the Malaysian ethnic Chinese to conceive of themselves as a coherent collective, and yet, when asked, Chinese entrepreneurs maintain that despite the affirmative action policy ethnicity is not a deciding factor when it comes to identifying business partners.

This book focuses on the consequences of these kinds of policies in the field of inter-ethnic business practices and entrepreneurship in Malaysia within the wider context of the relationship between local, national and global markets. It focuses on the complexities of inter-ethnic relations and in particular, the strong economic position of the ethnic Chinese and their impact on the Malaysian economic scene as well as on the wider Southeast Asian region, underlining the degree to which inter-ethnic relations in Southeast Asia are crucial to understanding the political and economic complexities characterising the region. In turn, it takes small and medium-sized enterprises as case studies, and shows how they are being shaped and in return shape the society in which they constitute a part. In doing so, this book highlights how these companies not only relate to the domestic economy, but also cater to the global economy, and presents a compelling argument for the introduction of a glocalised perspective in international business studies.

Ethnic Chinese Entrepreneurship in Malaysia will be welcomed by students and scholars with an interest in Asian studies, political economy, international business studies, inter-ethnic relations and diaspora studies.

Michael Jakobsen is an associate professor in the Department of International Economics and Management at Copenhagen Business School, Denmark.

Chinese Worlds

Chinese Worlds publishes high-quality scholarship, research monographs, and source collections on Chinese history and society. 'Worlds' signals the diversity of China, the cycles of unity and division through which China's modern history has passed, and recent research trends toward regional studies and local issues. It also signals that Chineseness is not contained within borders – ethnic migrant communities overseas are also 'Chinese worlds'.

The series editors are Gregor Benton, Flemming Christiansen, Delia Davin, Terence Gomez and Hong Liu.

1. **The Literary Fields of Twentieth-Century China**
   Edited by Michel Hockx

2. **Chinese Business in Malaysia**
   Accumulation, ascendance, accommodation
   Edmund Terence Gomez

3. **Internal and International Migration**
   Chinese perspectives
   Edited by Frank N. Pieke and Hein Mallee

4. **Village Inc.**
   Chinese rural society in the 1990s
   Edited by Flemming Christiansen and Zhang Junzuo

5. **Chen Duxiu's Last Articles and Letters, 1937–1942**
   Edited and translated by Gregor Benton

6. **Encyclopedia of the Chinese Overseas**
   Edited by Lynn Pan

7. **New Fourth Army**
   Communist resistance along the Yangtze and the Huai, 1938–1941
   Gregor Benton

8. **A Road is Made**
   Communism in Shanghai 1920–1927
   Steve Smith

9. **The Bolsheviks and the Chinese Revolution 1919–1927**
   Alexander Pantsov

10. **Chinas Unlimited**
    Gregory Lee

11. **Friend of China – The Myth of Rewi Alley**
    Anne-Marie Brady

Ethnic Chinese Entrepreneurship in Malaysia

On contextualisation in international business studies

Michael Jakobsen

Routledge
Taylor & Francis Group

LONDON AND NEW YORK

First published 2015 by Routledge

2 Park Square, Milton Park, Abingdon, Oxon OX14 4RN
711 Third Avenue, New York, NY 10017, USA

Routledge is an imprint of the Taylor & Francis Group, an informa business

First issued in paperback 2017

British Library Cataloguing in Publication Data

A catalogue record for this book is available from the British Library

Library of Congress Cataloging-in-Publication Data

Jakobsen, Michael, author.
   Ethnic Chinese entrepreneurship in Malaysia : on contextualisation
in international business studies / Michael Jakobsen.
      pages cm. — (Chinese worlds ; 33)
   Includes bibliographical references and index.
   1. Chinese—Commerce—Malaysia.   2. Chinese—Malaysia—Economic
conditions.   3. Entrepreneurship—Malaysia.   4. Corporations,
Chinese—Malaysia.   5. Malaysia—Ethnic relations.   I. Title.
   HF3800.6.Z5J33 2015
   338'.040899510595—dc23
   2014023301

ISBN: 978-1-138-81872-9 (hbk)
ISBN: 978-1-138-10417-4 (pbk)

Typeset in Times New Roman
by Apex CoVantage, LLC

Contents

Figures

Tables

Introduction

The study of ethnic Chinese in Southeast Asia has a long tradition. Anthropologists, sociologists and political scientists, as well as economists, have produced a substantial number of books and articles on this particular ethnic group. When going through the literature, the first thing that strikes the reader is how difficult it is to generalise about this ethnic group in the region. Even though there seems to be many different kinds of relations between them binding them together, it is not the same as saying that they relate to each other because of the fact that they share the same ethnic background. Even though they thus constitute a very heterogeneous ethnic group it is interesting to notice how they have been allowed or not allowed to be Chinese down through the political history of especially Indonesia and Malaysia because of different processes of social and political engineering that make them more or less distinct as an ethnic group.

Zooming further in on especially Malaysia, which constitutes the main empirical case in this book, what we see here is that national political schemes such as the affirmative action policy[1] indirectly force the Malaysian ethnic Chinese to conceive of themselves as a coherent ethnic group. On the basis of this, this book argues, together with Yao, that if ethnic groups and ethnically linked networks do exist, then they are externally and not internally constructed. That is, they are artefacts of forces from the outside, not love from the inside. Thus, ethnic networks are born out of distrust rather than trust. To go a step further, it is possible to argue that networks are formed by ethnic Chinese from a position of weakness, not strength. As a result the affirmative action policies as enacted in Malaysia produce a certain kind of societal alienation on behalf of the ethnic Chinese. In light of this, ethnic based groups and networks can be conceptualised as a group strategy – not to build trust per se, but rather to cope with distrust (Yao 2002b).

This book focuses on the consequences of these kinds of policies in the field of inter-ethnic business practices and entrepreneurship in Malaysia. Interestingly, when applying this issue on ethnic Chinese entrepreneurs in the state of Penang, they maintain that despite the affirmative action policy it is not ethnicity that is the defining factor when identifying business partners. As they see it, it is what kind of opportunities other businessmen, regardless of ethnic background, can provide. These kinds of statements deal a severe blow to that part of the international discourse on ethnic Chinese business practices that identifies them as part and parcel of ethnically dominated types of networks, described in the business literature as tribe-like or constituting bamboo networks or underground empires, based on diasporic linkages that, according to, for example, Fukuyama (1995), Redding (1996) and Ong and Nonini (1997), typify Chinese business practices and entrepreneurship.

Political engineered or stereotypical perceptions of ethnic Chinese entrepreneurship do thus not work when relating actual Chinese business practices and entrepreneurship to a given societal context – in this case the Malaysian one – because of the dynamic economic relationship between the global and local levels. Taking this argument further, this book maintains that it is more fruitful to construct a triangular relationship that consists of global business practices, the Malaysian national business context and the societal context in which the two other points in the triangle are embedded when studying ethnic Chinese entrepreneurship and business practices. The point here is thus not focusing the research on inter-ethnic bonding within business but rather on the processes between the different points in the triangle which together identify the entrepreneurs as either partners or competitors, who operate in a given business context.

One of the key approaches taken in this book, when studying this triangle and the relationship between the three constituent points, is international business studies. Here social and political engineered perception of entrepreneurship is taken out of the equation and during the theoretical studies turned into more or less anonymous agents, who act according to a relatively narrow defined mode of being identified as either bounded rational and/or opportunistic inclined agents. It is only in the application of this theoretical approach on a given empirical context that agents are (re-)turned into social and political motivated agents because of the impact from various societal factors. On the basis of this explanatory frameworks are thus being created so as to facilitate a study of ethnic Chinese entrepreneurship based on a combination of international business studies and grounded theory.

The main aim of this book is to suggest various modes of probing deeper into a given national institutional framework in which ethnic Chinese entrepreneurs work to test the explanatory power of the different theoretical models employed in international business studies, either from a firm-specific or from a generic market perspective. To facilitate such an approach, this book is divided into four parts.

Part I focuses on the global context. It is argued that it is imperative to identify which approach to understanding the global economy is the most appropriate in this connection. Four different approaches on how to read the global economy are presented. The first one, a so-called decoupling approach, focuses on whether it is possible to decouple from the current global economy. Here the main finding is that with continuous integration of the national economies into the global economy, decoupling from the global economy is very problematic if not impossible because of increasing interdependency and harmonisation of the different national economies, which are gradually transforming themselves into a transnational economic web. The weak aspect of this perspective is that it does not take into account the impacts of local societal factors.

The second approach on the global economy likewise does not take local impacts into account. Here the main focus is on how to visualise the global economy. Is it 'flat' or 'spiky'? If it is flat, then the global economy is approaching full integration and harmonisation of the different national economies, thus standardising economic practices in the different types of markets. This perception of the global economy is disputed and thus a counter perception has been forwarded: that the world is divided into various kinds of 'spikes', 'hills' and 'valleys', representing different levels of economic activity. Local specificities in this context are reduced to set pieces ready to fit into a frame that is conditioned according to whether we are talking about 'spikes', 'hills' or 'valleys'.

The third approach is a typical international business view of the global economy. Here the global economy is divided into three main types of markets: developed markets, emerging markets and bottom-of-the-pyramid (BOP) markets. It is a categorisation that is currently losing its explanatory power as the different types of markets merge into one another because of increasingly complex integration and capitalisation of the three types of markets. A good case in point is Asia, where all three types of markets exist and are gradually merging, thus making navigation of these markets a very complex task.

The fourth and in this context final approach to thinking about the global economy can be described as a 'glocalised' perception of the relationship between the global and local economies. Thus, global developments, including political and social as well as economic ones, cannot be disentangled from a given local context. The key word when discussing glocalisation is *context;* context matters in all aspects of the global community. According to this perspective, it is not possible to disentangle the local market from the global one; they condition each other through a complex web of interdependencies, thus blurring their individual points of reference. This last approach is the one employed in this book. To illustrate this approach, triangulation is applied so as to relate the global economy, a national economy and a local economy in which the first two points – the global and the national – intersect with each other and with the third – the local economy. The triangle thus constitutes a matrix in which all three constituent points play themselves out.

In Part II, the perspective moves from the global scene to a regional one, more specifically the Southeast Asian region. Having identified glocalisation as the perspective most suitable for understanding the global economy, we now zoom in on a region to approach a less abstract level of context. Here the links between the global and the regional are fleshed out to show and stress the interdependencies between the two. In the Southeast Asian region, the focus is further narrowed down to Malaysia, the setting for the empirical discussion in this book. An international business analysis on Malaysian market conditions is then initiated, framed in Dunning's (2000) eclectic paradigm and North's (1991) and Scott's (2010) interpretations of institutional theory, thus providing an approach to this market from both a firm-specific and a generic market perspective.

After having provided an overall perspective of the Malaysian market, in both a regional and domestic environment, the final contextual focus in this book, the Malaysian state of Penang, is introduced. Here the local social organisation as well as the state government's economic policies are described, together with some socio-economic facilitators that the government and government-linked organisations are using to further develop the state's industrial environment to help the national economy move up the global value chain.

When probing further into the Malaysian economy, one specific feature quickly becomes obvious, namely the complexities of inter-ethnic relations and in particular the strong economic position of the ethnic Chinese and their impact on the Malaysian economic scene. As this feature is not confined to Malaysia, a discussion of the position of the ethnic Chinese in Southeast Asia is provided. This provides the necessary background to understand the importance of an intricate regional inter-ethnic puzzle in which the Chinese ethnic minority is the major economic stakeholder, as opposed to other majority ethnic groups, not only in Malaysia, but throughout the region. On the whole, inter-ethnic relations in Southeast Asia are key to understanding the political and economic complexities characteristic of this region. Without this background knowledge, many of the local drivers behind the social and institutional arrangements, both formal and informal, cannot be identified or understood.

Part III zooms further in on the local context within Malaysia. It is divided into two main sections. The first section focuses on the inter-ethnic relations in Malaysian society. The relationship between ethnic groups is one of the main drivers behind the society and helps us understand how this nation remains a coherent entity. This discussion is based on political positions from the dominant political establishment, represented by two of Malaysia's prime ministers, Mahathir Mohamad, who governed the country from 1981 to 2003, and Mohd Najib Abdul Razak, who became prime minister in 2009. This overview provides us with insights into how seriously different Malaysian governments, past and present, take the question of inter-ethnic relations.

The second section is based on three case studies of small and medium-sized enterprises (SMEs) in the automation industry. These case studies do not focus on the individual companies themselves, but rather on how they are being shaped and in return shape the society in which they constitute a part. The reason for choosing this type of company in the context of a book on international business studies is that these companies not only relate to the domestic economy, but also cater to the global economy. Two of them are subcontractors to multinational corporations (MNCs) and two of them are international in their own right as a consequence of the dual nature of the Malaysian economy, that is, an economy that is divided into private and semi-public private sectors with little overlap between the two main categories.

Seen from an international business studies perspective, a combination of generic and firm-specific theoretical models provides a potential investor with crucial information on whether to invest in Penang in particular, or more broadly, in the Malaysian economy. At this point, however, we are beginning to move beyond what an international business approach is capable of excavating in terms of drivers behind the institutions on which this society is based. The current book argues for introducing the notion of a glocalised perspective in international business studies. This combines an etic research approach with an emic research approach, thereby introducing a new perspective on how to analyse the Malaysian market and economy in general.

Part IV uses the main findings from the previous chapters to demonstrate the impact of the global economy on the local one and vice versa. Here we are talking about a fragmentation of the local market due to impacts from the global economy, which leads to intense local competition, thus increasing the pressure on the structural development of the local market, thus facilitating the development of economic fault-lines in the process. One of these fault-lines has been identified as the so-called middle income trap, where the development of the economy has come to a halt, as it cannot advance to the next level of economic development, which is characterised as being innovation-driven. This middle income trap characterises the current Malaysian economy, stuck in the confines of manufacturing, although manufacturing on a very high level.

The final part of this book discusses various initiatives to move beyond this situation, mainly based on how the local automation industry defines innovation as the main driver to lift Malaysia, both its society and industry, out of the current middle income trap. This discussion argues for the imperative of stressing the contextual aspect in international business studies even more. Generic economic studies are of course necessary when dealing with the complexities of the different markets, but these studies must be accompanied by a deep knowledge of the local societal context. For an investor to feel secure investing large sums in a foreign market it is imperative to be able to identify the main drivers behind that particular market. In the Malaysian context it is important to know, for example, whether Chinese business practices really are ethnically determined, as often stated in the academic literature on cross-cultural business practices, or whether such business practices are determined by more general social and political forces within the society in question. Questions such as these constitute the essence of what this book is trying to convey. The ultimate aim is to encourage international business scholars to probe even deeper into the societal environment, thus contributing to expanding the explanatory power of international business studies further.

Note

1 For details on this policy see Chapters 4 and 5.

Part I
The global context

1   Visualising the global economy

When discussing the current global financial crisis, two striking features are the externalisation of the strong links between international financial markets and the inability of national economies to shield their domestic markets from the negative effects of the international crisis. Combining these two features underlines the fact that the global community consists of nation-states that are bound together in a political and economic community characterised by interdependency and processes of global political and economic integration.

This movement towards an increasing interdependency and internationalisation of domestic economies does not necessarily lead to a harmonious and stable global community, as can be seen by the current difference between Western and Asian markets. As for now, the former are performing at nearly recession level, whereas the latter are experiencing annual growth rates on average of around 5 to 6 per cent; China and India have growth rates rather close to double digits, namely 7.8 and 6.5 per cent respectively.[1]

Does this difference between Western and Asian markets allow Asian markets, at least temporarily, to disengage from their troubled Western counterparts in order to nurture their own developmental potential? This chapter explores the viability of disengagement by taking a critical look at the discourse of decoupling. It then proceeds to present an alternative perspective on the global economy by introducing the notion of 'spiky' and 'flat' economies. This notion of how to think about the global economy centres on whether to employ a multidimensional or a one-dimensional approach to the global economy. A multidimensional perspective argues that the global economic landscape consists of 'spikes', 'hills' and 'valleys'. The one-dimensional view sees an evening out of national economic differences due to a global standardisation of financial transactions and production processes, thus the global economy is seen to be gradually becoming more streamlined throughout the world.

After critiquing both the decoupling perspective and the notion of a spiky or flat global economy, this chapter moves on to introduce an affiliated approach to analysing the global economy, this time based on market differentiation as employed within international business studies. According to this approach, the global economy is based on three main types of markets: developed markets, emerging markets and the so-called bottom-of-the-pyramid (BOP) markets. In this approach the main determining factors are the level of institutionalisation of the economy and the role of the state.

A fourth and final approach to analysing the global economy is based on a so-called glocalised mode of perceiving the global economic landscape. The term *glocalisation* was coined in the late 1980s to emphasise that the globalisation of a product is more likely to succeed when the product or service is adapted to a specific locality or culture in which it is marketed. The main mantra in this context is 'think global, act local'. Out of these four approaches, the last has been selected as the main approach to be used as the lens through which the case study in this book, the Southeast Asian nation-state Malaysia, is analysed.

1.1   Decoupling: real possibility or intellectual exercise?

The intellectual roots behind the notion of decoupling can be found in the Dependency School that dominated mainstream political and economic discourse during the 1960s, 1970s and 1980s, with its thesis that the world is divided into a so-called First World and a Third World political and economic power structure. The theoretical foundation behind this bifocal view of the world was based mainly on neo-Marxist approaches formulated by scholars such as Emmanuel (1972), Amir (1974), Banaji (1977), Frank (1978) and Wallerstein (1979).

The point of departure for this school of thought was the political and economic processes that had their origin in a Western colonial and imperialist past, which then manifested themselves in a global centre–periphery relationship in which the centre, the West, monopolised and controlled capital accumulation fuelled by resource extraction in the periphery, that is, all countries outside the West, mainly in Latin America and Africa. The link to the discourse on decoupling was provided by Frank, who maintained that so-called Third World countries should de-link from the First World for their economic development, as these links were harmful for the periphery. With fewer linkages to the centre, Third World countries could concentrate on domestic development and import substitution, all guided by a developmental state based on a revolutionary socialist ideology (Frank 1978).

This theoretical macro perspective was later replaced by theories of globalisation in which multinational companies were the main players and nation-states acted as economic facilitators for domestic industrial internationalisation processes, developments that in particular have been discussed within international business theory by Porter (1990), Rugman and Verbeke (2004), Shenkar (2004) and Dunning and Lundan (2009), just to mention a few scholars in this rich field of research. Up until 2008, observers found supportive evidence for budding notions of decoupling, especially in Asian emerging markets. A good case in point is the discourse on 'Asian values' during the 1970s, 1980s and early 1990s (see for example Jakobsen and Bruun 2000), and again after the Asian financial crisis in 1997, that showed tremendous economic growth rates, especially in China and India, and much higher growth rates in the rest of East and Southeast Asia compared to the Western economies. As such, Asian economies were perceived as resistant to the contractions in the American and European economies because of their strong and constantly growing domestic markets, large currency reserves and prudent macroeconomic policies, partly based on experiences learnt during the 1997 financial crisis and partly based on perceived modes of doing business compared to their Western counterparts.[2]

During 2008 and 2009, however, cracks in the notion of decoupling began to emerge. The meltdown on Wall Street in 2008 sent shockwaves through the entire global financial system, not least in the Asian markets. Contrary to what those who believed in decoupling expected, the losses were even greater outside the United States, with the worst experienced in emerging markets and developed economies such as Germany and Japan.[3] Even though China was relatively hard hit by the global economic contraction that followed the financial meltdown, it managed to engineer a decent rebound (together with India and a group of larger emerging economies in Asia), whereas the United States, Europe and Japan remain on the verge of recession. In the first half of 2011 it seemed as if the global economy was approaching the second bottom of a seemingly 'W-shaped' (also called 'double dip') economic crisis.

Taking into account the many fiscal stimulus packages introduced by states in 2009 and 2010 to stabilise national economies around the globe, it seems at least for the time being that those in Asian economies have had the greatest impact on national economies, thus rejuvenating an otherwise rather battered discourse on regional or national modes of decoupling. However, the main question remains whether the current growth of the Asian economies is a sign of a budding decoupling from the global economy, and in particular from Western economies. It is still too early to tell, as we do not know whether the current recovery will be sustained once the effects of the massive stimulus packages begin to fade.

A critical point when analysing these developments from a decoupling perspective is the relationship between decoupling and the underlying process of internationalisation of individual national economies. Even though a given national economy has been stimulated and facilitated in its development by the state, it does not mean that the economy is becoming detached from the global economy. Evidence of continuing links between a national economy and the global economy can be seen in a national economy's dependence on foreign direct investment (FDI) for its continued growth and through membership of the World Trade Organisation (WTO), for example. In this way, the state is gradually aligning the development of its own economy with the global one.[4] Turning to political decoupling, the Association of Southeast Asian Nations (ASEAN) has tried this through its developmental regionalism experiment, initiated in 1998. That experience ended in 2001 because of heavy criticism by the major global economic players as an attempt to introduce differentiated levels of competitiveness between the national, regional and global levels, thus damaging the free flow of capital between them (Nesadurei 2004).

Thus, it is problematic to employ the notion of decoupling, as global and local linkages remain strong and pervasive. It seems as if the discourse on decoupling is not aware of the current gradual dismantling of the historically conditioned

Western economic hegemony, a condition that is being replaced by a more fluid, interdependent and contextualised economic world order based on shifting centres of capital accumulation. Asia is a very good case in point (and China and India in particular), taking the current developments in this region into consideration. Decoupling or recoupling, if we are to use these terms at all, seem to be less economic in nature and more part of a politically inspired discourse in which the notions of decoupling or recoupling constitute potent political signifiers. Taking this stand on decoupling reduces it to a domestic policy manifestation that reflects a given position in an international landscape of multiple and shifting power centres, thereby unintentionally accepting an increasing global interdependency between and harmonisation of individual national economies (Rugman and Verbeke 2004).

1.2   Beyond decoupling: towards a 'spiky' or 'flat' perception of the global economy?

Before introducing an alternative approach to analysing the relationship between economic globalisation and national economies, it is important to take a closer look at the current global political and economic landscape to identify the various opportunities and constraints that are impacting the economies in the Asian region. Based on a geo-economic understanding of the global economy, Thomas L. Friedman, in his book, *The World Is Flat: A Brief History of the Twenty-First Century* (2005), put forward the notion of a flat world as a metaphor for seeing the world economy as an increasingly level playing field. This means that agents in the global marketplace have an equal opportunity in terms of doing business. Friedman based this presumption on what he has identified as 'the ten flatteners',[5] which combined with the so-called steroids[6] and the triple global convergence[7] have all led towards greater global interdependency. According to Friedman, the net result of these developments has been a gradual alignment of doing business in the global marketplace especially in the beginning of the twenty-first century.

Because of the so-called time-space compression (Harvey 1990: 240), that is, processes that merge or collapse the difference between time and space, inter- and intra-firm communication tends to be instantaneous. Accordingly, adaptation to local market and institutional conditions becomes an option and not a necessity for a global company. The Nobel Prize-winning economist Joseph Stiglitz has been rather critical of Friedman's notion of a flat world and thus also of the notion and consequences of time-space compression. In his 2006 book, *Making Globalization Work,* he writes:

> Friedman is right that there have been dramatic changes in the global economy, in the global landscape; in some directions, the world is much flatter than it has ever been, with those in various parts of the world being more connected than they have ever been, but the world is not flat. . . . Not only is the world not flat: in many ways it has been getting less flat.
>
> (Stiglitz 2006: 7)

Richard Florida (2005), from George Mason University, concurred with Stiglitz that the world is not flat, but 'spiky'. According to Florida, the world can be divided into three major categories that together make up the modern economic landscape: 'spikes', that is, cities that generate innovations, economic production 'hills' and the 'valleys' in between the two. To illustrate this, he and some colleagues developed a map that shows geo-economically what a 'spiky world' would look like. The map illustrates economic activity estimated on the basis of light emissions. Many cities, despite their large populations, barely register because of low levels of economic activity. The 'spikes' or cities that are capable of generating technological innovations constitute the tallest peaks on this map and are rather permanent. They attract global talent and create new products and industries.

The 'economic hills' are manufacturing centres that support the innovation engines found in the 'spikes'. The hills can rise and fall quickly; they are prosperous but insecure in terms of investment. Finally, there are the 'valleys', which can be found in between the 'spikes' and 'hills'. These are places or areas with little connection to the global economy and thus few immediate prospects for economic development. According to this geo-economic perspective, the world is not flat but constitutes a highly differentiated and interdependent landscape, if we are to believe these categorisations. To further substantiate the notion of a spiky world there are, however, more advanced ways of showing that a differentiated, interdependent and indeed 'spiky' economic landscape is closer to reality. One of these ways can be found in international business (IB) theory (Peng 2009; Ahlstrom and Bruton 2010; Peng and Meyer 2011). Besides showing that the various national economies are indeed interrelated and interdependent, theoretical approaches from this school of thought delineate various market types that are a direct reflection of the current forces defining the structure of the global economy.

1.3 From 'spiky' or 'flat' economies to differentiated market analyses

The IB approach has divided the global economy into three main types of markets: developed markets, transitional and/or emerging markets and BOP markets. The developed markets are those that contain the tallest 'spikes'. These markets generally can be found in what Fukuyama (1995) has called 'high-trust societies'. This refers to societies in which a high level of trust is placed in governmental institutions that provide for political accountability and checks and balances of the overall economy, as well as judicial protection and security for social groupings and individuals within civil society. In other words, these markets are defined by rules and regulations and as such attract a vast number of international and domestic investors.[8] Furthermore, the societies in which these markets are found can be characterised as exhibiting moderate growth rates and having stable political regimes.

The role of the state in developed markets can be organised into two main ideal types: liberal market economies (LMEs) and coordinated market economies

(CMEs).[9] In short, the role of the state in the LMEs can be characterised as minimal. This means that the state plays a minor role in regulating the market and ideally leaves the market to its own regulatory mechanisms with only minor interventions to stimulate the economy. In this category would be the US and UK markets, for example. This perception of the US and UK markets has temporarily changed because of the impact of the current financial crisis. The state has to a great extent increased its intervention in those two markets to facilitate an otherwise faltering economy.

However, there are heavy political costs associated with adopting this new practice of an interventionist state in an LME. This can be seen especially in the United States, where Republican politicians are heavily attacking the Obama administration for being 'socialist' in its approach to the current economic crisis, leading to a stalemate within the political establishment. In contrast, the role of the state in a CME can be categorised as Keynesian. Here the state plays a major role as an economic facilitator and regulator, a role that expands and contracts according to fluctuations in the market and the state of the economy. This kind of market is found mainly in Germany and Scandinavia. Both of these two ideal types of markets are within the developed market category.[10]

In transitional and/or emerging markets, one finds the 'hills'. They generally can be characterised as volatile. Some of these markets are going through a period of transition from a planned economy to an open market economy (for example, as Russia, China and Vietnam are currently doing), whereas other nations, together with the transitional economies, are based on more or less functioning formal rules and regulations because of the impact of localised mind-sets and traditional value systems. Other characteristics are high growth rates, very competitive low-cost manufacturing, high-risk economies and unstable political regimes. In general, the societies where one finds these types of markets can be defined as low-trust societies, to once again use Fukuyama's (1995) term. This means that individuals do not trust official institutions because of corruption and non-transparent political and bureaucratic practices, leading to inefficient implementation of the rules and regulations emanating from the formal institutions. Instead they turn to informal networks based on family relations and other non-official organised-centred networks built on relational trust between, for example, business partners.[11] In other words, contrary to formal institutions, informal institutions have a greater impact on the functionality of formal institutions, thus creating what Peng and Zhou (2005) have termed 'institutional voids' that are dealt with by network practices, which make up for the various institutional voids.

In terms of market characteristics, a transitional and/or emerging market can be positioned somewhere between an LME and a CME. This means that the role and involvement of the state in the economy is relatively high. The literature on the state in these kinds of markets refers to the state as either an interventionist state or a developmental state that to a great extent is involved in the economy and thus also in overall national industrial development (see for example Hutchinson 2009 and Beh 2007). Although variations of the developmental type of state can also be found in developed markets, it is mainly related to transitional and/or emerging markets, where market structures are relatively weak and unregulated, thus producing vulnerable industries that are easy prey for global competition. These kinds of markets can be found in Eastern Europe and Russia, Latin America, Africa, India and most of Asia except Japan, South Korea, Taiwan, Hong Kong and Singapore.

The final category of markets in this context is the so-called BOP type of markets. They constitute the 'valleys', using Florida's typology. They can be characterised by an absence of formal institutions, that is, of very few or no formal rules and regulations to guide either local or international companies doing business there. Here, informal rules can be understood as mainly socially sanctioned norms of behaviour that are embedded in cultural and religious practices as well as in local value systems. These markets are found mainly in rural areas, urban slums and shanty towns. People living in BOP markets have few assets, little or no education, are outside of conventional distribution, credit and communication networks, and they subsist on less than US$4 a day (Peng 2009: 6). BOP markets are scattered throughout the world, mostly in countries outside the West, for example, in parts of Latin America, Africa, India, China and Southeast Asia. One of the interesting things about BOP markets is that they have the potential to develop into emerging markets should the government invest in infrastructure, thus preparing the ground for companies other than MNCs to tap into these markets. The companies behind this kind of development are often successful pioneers who first established themselves in these difficult markets. Two such pioneers are Unilever Hindustan, which operates successfully in the Indian BOP market,[12] and the Danish company Fan Milk International A/S, which operates in several African countries.[13]

1.4 From a differentiated global market to a glocalised economy

According to Roland Robertson, who is credited with popularising the term, *glocalisation* describes the effects of local conditions on global pressures (Robertson 1995). Yale Ferguson and Richard Mansbach elaborate further on the concept, saying that the notion of glocalisation signifies the existence of complex 'parallel, irreversible and mutually interdependent processes by which globalisation-deepens-localisation-deepens-globalisation and so on' (Ferguson and Mansbach 2012: 138). The global and the local are thus inextricably and irreversibly bound together through a dynamic relationship with huge flows of resources moving backwards and forwards between the two. Neither the global nor the local exists without the other.[14]

The key issue here is what has been termed the *global-local nexus,* or to use a more popular phrase, 'think globally, act locally'. The different types of markets, whether spiky or flat, whether you can decouple or not, are all governed by the global-local nexus, that is, the global impact on the local and vice versa. As it is the interface between the two that determines the success rate at either the global or local level, we must take a closer look at this interface to understand what it consists of and identify the drivers behind it. Basically, it is this interface that constitutes the complex reality 'out there' that we have to deal with in our every-day life.

As glocalisation not only deals with economic matters but encompasses all aspects of the local in the global, it is important to look at the main players in this context, which can be grouped in a triangular matrix. The individual points in this matrix consist of 1) global political and economic developments, 2) the role of the state and 3) the civil society. By analysing the relationships among these three main players it becomes possible to identify the drivers behind glocalisation. When employing such an approach, the intricate interdependency between a given region (in this particular case, Southeast Asia), a particular nation (Malaysia) and a specific locality (the state of Penang) clearly comes forth. The following discussion of the implications of employing the notion of glocalisation amounts to a holistic approach to analysing the triangle, as we recognise that the three other modes of thinking about the global economy – decoupling, spiky or flat or a qualitative market differentiation – only address two of the corners in the triangle, namely the global political and economic developments and the role of the state. On the basis of this critique we begin our discussion by taking a closer look at the way the main players in the triangular matrix relate to each other.

It is possible to argue that the fluidity that permeates the contemporary international community is driven especially by political and economic globalisation, the aggregated effect of which has a huge impact on the relationship between the nation and the state. As the individual nation-state increasingly depends on the international community for its economic survival exemplified by its quest for FDI, this dependency on the global economy has as one consequence that it rolls back aspects of national sovereignty, thus gradually opening up the national hinterland to more international influences. These developments initiate a process of disaggregating state and nation, where a gradual disarticulation of the relationship between state and nation produces new societal spaces, which are contested by non-statist interest groups and transnational, de-territorialised, ethnic-affiliated groups and networks. It has been argued in this connection that, for example, Southeast Asian ethnic Chinese use these newly created spaces to set up diasporic networks, thus providing substance for transnational ethno-scapes (Appadurai 1991) or nations without states (Ohmae 1995).

Such a reading of current affairs in an ever more global world leads to a view that global processes are omnipotent and simultaneously local and global in scope. The contemporary world can thus be characterised as displaying a high degree of time-space compression that allows us to immediately acknowledge different types of events regardless of where in the world they take place (Harvey 1990). It is this conception of immediacy that governs this author's perception of glocalisation. I use this view during the following discussion of the relationship between a budding disaggregation of nation and state, changing perceptions of citizenship and transnational migration framed in more or less diasporic networks. In this context, special emphasis will be put on the ethnic Chinese in Southeast Asia.

1.5 The changing contemporary nation-state

Just as perceptions of the extent of the world have changed down through history so have the conceptions and constitution of the (nation) state. Arguably, one has to distinguish between the main raison d'être for pre-modern and modern types of states. Pre-modern states were mostly concerned with controlling trade routes and making political alliances with more or less collaborative cultures in a fluid and difficult to control political landscape. Modern states, linking their legitimacy to managing a specific geographic area, are obsessed with policing national borders, maintaining state sovereignty, self-determination and non-interference in an international community generally thought of as consisting of predatory fellow states.

The origin of the modern state is generally attributed to the Treaty of Westphalia in 1648, but it was only after the commencement of the industrial revolution in eighteenth-century Europe that the state evolved into its present form, that is, towards a state with a precisely defined national territory. Historically speaking, the notion and construction of the modern nation-state is thus relatively recent. For example, the embryonic establishment of the Southeast Asian states only took off during the late colonial period and the contemporary Asian version of the modern nation-state only began to establish itself during the transition from colonial to independent (nation) states in the mid twentieth century. This type of state differs markedly from pre-colonial forms of 'states' in the region, as they were either based on collaboration between one or two sultanates or consisted of fragile alliances between a sultanate and tribal-like chieftainships kept together by political and military relations backed by elaborate trade networks (see Reid 1993). The contemporary perception of antiquity and thus permanency attributed to the modern Asian nation-state is thus based on atavistic-inspired ideological references to such sultanates and chieftainships, thereby unwittingly underscoring their own truncated life span and political and ideological attempts to legitimate their current form and function.

The 'classical' conception of the contemporary nation-state in particular can be allotted to the period after World War II, which entails, according to the realist school in international relations theory, a perception of the state as an almost absolutist and total sovereign entity (Krasner 1999). Robert Jackson (1990) writes that the sovereignty that such a state ascribes to is to be perceived as a legal, absolute and unitary condition. It is legal in that a sovereign state is not subordinate to another sovereign, but is necessarily equal to it by international law – although not necessarily in fact. It is absolute in that sovereignty is either present or absent. When a country is sovereign it is independent categorically: there is no intermediate condition. It is unitary in that a sovereign state is a supreme authority within its own jurisdiction. This is the case whether a state has a unitary or a federal constitution, because in either case it is the sole authority in its external relations with other states (Jackson 1990: 32). Thus, the state is the sole and ultimate organiser of the national community.

A much-used way of further knitting the relationship between nation and state together is to construct a nationalist-inspired societal membrane between nations, thus creating the necessary 'other' in terms of national self-identification. This is done, for example, by imposing specific notions of citizenship that automatically exclude anyone who does not fall into the state's defined categories. Stephen Castles and Alastair Davidson (2000) emphasise three main types of citizenship:

- *ius sanguinis:* citizenship is based on ethnicity or an ideologically constructed folk model that operates on the notion of descent from a national from within the country concerned when electability for citizenship is determined;
- *ius soli:* citizenship is based on multiple ethnic groups where birth in the territory of the country in question is more important than descent from citizens within a legitimate national ethnic group;
- *ius domicile:* this is a rather new way of gaining entitlement to citizenship as it is possible to achieve through mere residence in the national territory. It has also been referred to as a *law of residence* by some analysts.

According to Castles and Davidson, colonial powers usually introduced the nationality rules that existed for their own subjects in their colonies. This meant that throughout the British and American empires, *ius soli* became law, while in French and Dutch possessions a combination of *ius soli* and a modified *ius sanguinis* was typically established (Castles and Davidson 2000: 190).

The three ways of achieving citizenship refer to different categories of societies even though they are all based on the classical notion of the nation-state defined earlier. Citizenship defined along *ius sanguinis* lines makes it extremely difficult for non-nationals to achieve citizenship if they do not have a relative in the pertinent nation. And if they do, but these relatives were not born in the nation, then it is still difficult to achieve citizenship. In this case it is completely up to the discretion of the individual state to grant a non-native citizenship, which gives the state a high degree of control over who becomes a citizen. All ethnic groups that have been incorporated into these states after independence thus face immense obstacles in terms of jobs, education, health care, political rights and so forth, as they are not regarded as original to the nation and thus not automatically entitled to citizenship. As a generic definition, states using this criterion for citizenship can be termed *ethnocratic states,* as they base themselves on one or a small core of dominating (ethnic) group(s). According to Barry Sautman, an ethnocracy is:

a descriptor for a regime that expresses the identity and aspirations of one ethnic group in an ethnically divided society, based on rule over other ethnic groups who are accorded only qualified rights to citizenship. Ethnocracy's reason d'etre is to secure the key instruments of state power for the dominant ethnic collectivity; it allows only those facets of democracy consistent with the demos being identical with that group and not the collective population.

(Sautman 2002: 3)

According to Castles and Davidson (2000), countries based on principles close to *ius sanguinis* and ethnocracies are Papua New Guinea, Fiji, Indonesia, Malaysia, Burma, Vietnam, South Korea, Taiwan, Japan and China.

In relation to countries that have adopted the *ius soli* principle, it is much easier to obtain citizenship. Castles and Davidson note that all nations that fall into this category are multi-ethnic, with both indigenous minorities and a large population of foreign labourers. Such states may be regarded as highly progressive because of the porousness of their citizenship rules, which make them clearly distinguishable from the former colonies, which have reversed the British and American *ius soli* rules in favour of *ius sanguinis* ones. Of countries in the *ius soli* category we find Australia, New Zealand, India, Singapore and the Philippines (Castles and Davidson 2000: 190–191).

Finally, *ius domicile* is generally combined with one of the two other main categories of citizenship. Paradoxically, according to Castles and Davidson, those countries that base their citizenship rules on *ius sanguinis* experiment most with *ius domicile* rules as a supplement to the general rules of *ius sanguinis*. The main idea behind this is to provide young people of immigrant origin with an option to become citizens. This development has a footing in a cynical calculation that exclusion from citizenship is problematic, leading to social marginalisation, political exclusion, conflict and racism. This experiment is thus born out of a need to preserve social and political stability (Castles and Davidson 2000: 193–194).

Most if not all nations in the Asia Pacific region are thus based more or less exclusively on either *ius sanguinis* or *ius soli* principles, as they provide the state with strong tools for controlling the flow of people in and out of the nation. It is only in regional organisations such as the European Union (EU) that serious experiments with *ius domicile* have taken place. The reason for this is likewise cynical as the increasing incorporation of nation-states into a more integrated union has made this development imperative. This has meant a gradual easing of restrictions on citizenship among EU citizens to facilitate labour mobility and migration within the union, a mobility that is essential as the individual states develop at different rates.

As the Asia Pacific region does not yet have this kind of political and economic integration, the imperative for incorporating *ius domicile* principles in its notions of citizenship has not arisen. The current development of regionalism is generally a statist-driven process that has so far resulted in the formation of the Asia Free Trade Area (AFTA), Asia-Pacific Economic Cooperation (APEC), Association of Southeast Asian Nations – Australia (ASEAN+1) and Association of Southeast Asian Nations – China, Japan, South Korea (ASEAN+3), all based on principles of non-intervention in the internal affairs of the individual member states. This non-intervention principle fits especially well with the ASEAN countries, as it reinforces their efforts to jealously safeguard their relatively newly won sovereignty. I return to this in a later section when discussing the difference between regionalism and regionalisation and what this means for questions concerning citizenship and national coherence in terms of a budding disaggregation of nation and state.

1.6   Expanding globalisation and contracting nation-states

The question now is whether this close relationship between concepts of citizenship, sovereignty, state, nation and principles of regionalism is still possible in an international community that has become much more complex, interconnected and volatile during the past three decades. The reason for this scepticism is that various processes of globalisation, especially those dealing with the increasing transnational mobility of finance capital, telecommunications technology and transportation, have gradually become more entrenched nationally, thereby strengthening the internationally oriented network already established there.

Elaborating on the economic aspect of globalisation, Hans-Henrik Holm and Georg Sørensen (1995) advance a scenario in which distinct national economies are subsumed and re-articulated into the global finance system by essentially international processes and transactions. Domestic politics, whether those of private corporations or public regulators, now routinely have to take into account the international flow of capital in their sphere of operations. The national is thus permeated and transformed by the international. Holm and Sørensen furthermore maintain that true economic globalisation invokes a qualitative shift towards a global economic system that is no longer based on autonomous national economies but on a consolidated global marketplace for production, distribution and consumption. According to this perspective, the global economy dominates national economies existing within it (Holm and Sørensen 1995: 5).

Holm and Sørensen wrote this almost twenty years ago, but their description of the ongoing processes of economic globalisation fits perfectly into the current notion of glocalisation. It portrays an international community in which nation-states are no longer capable of controlling the internal flow of capital because of the transnational organisation of those flows. The scenario offered by neo-realists such as Kenneth Waltz (2008) of contemporary processes of globalisation does not, it seems, explain the dynamics behind the rapidly changing international environment. Nation-states are gradually becoming disempowered when implementing rules and regulations to manage economic transactions. The international community represented by the WTO, for instance, is forcing states to abide by international standards when enacting domestic economic policies. Furthermore, the previously fixed nature of centres of capital control has been transformed into multiple and shifting centres of capital accumulation. The East and Southeast Asian tiger and dragon economies, centres of capital accumulation before the economic crisis hit them in July 1997, together with the current rising economic might of China and India, stand in stark contrast to the continuing problems that the United States and Europe, the traditional centres of capital accumulation, are currently facing. The contemporary era of globalisation is thus characterised by shifting capital centres, as the global economy has become highly mobile and resistant to statist regulations and national borders.

The contemporary nation-states have seen their room for manoeuvring confined by this new economic order. This has entailed a hollowing out of their sovereignty as the International Monetary Fund, Asia Development Bank, World Bank, World

Trade Organisation, International Labour Organisation and the United Nations have demanded that states accede to and incorporate international political and economic conventions and regulations when designing national political and economic policies. In case a state violates the agreed-upon international conventions and regulations, sanctions are imposed to force compliance. The main purpose of these sanctions is to reintegrate the errant state into the international community, as it still forms part of that community, despite breaches. Arguably, there is no room for non-complying nation-states outside of the international community as the latter encompasses the whole globe.

Paradoxically, these international political initiatives, reinforced by economic globalisation, also has empowered various ethnic groups within a national territory, thereby enabling them to mount pressure on the state to grant them recognition, from political autonomy to cultural respect. For example, a budding supranational morality framed in universal human rights agendas has created space for ethnic groups to promote issues on an international level, which could initiate qualitative shifts in the conditions of people's lives at the local level (Holm and Sørensen 1995: 5; Castles and Davidson 2000: 204; see also Friedman 1998: 1–20). The same is true for a wide range of non-governmental organisations (NGOs).

Rephrased, it is possible to argue that various aspects of globalisation are leading to an assertive resurgence of local identities, thereby producing an increasing social and political awareness within ethnic groups, making them influential players in the national political power game. Furthermore, globalisation is encouraging this development by supporting the emergence of a supranational moral construct based on an adherence to a universal human rights regime together with the implementation of notions of good governance and transparent democracy. Admittedly, this seems highly hypothetical when current international affairs, governed as they are by predatory neo-liberal strategies and total American political, economic and military hegemony, dictate a partial return to earlier anarchic periods in the international community. How the international community will deal with this latter development is still to be seen. Perhaps the solution is not to be sought in the political realm but rather in the economic imperatives that the global economy is forcing on the individual nation-states.

Put together, the dual effects of globalisation, that is, international intervention and local empowerment within the national sphere, which constitute the beginning and end in an interrelated movement, is perhaps a more precise definition of glocalisation than the one forwarded by Robertson (1995) and Ferguson and Mansbach (2012) respectively. Friedman (1998) has termed it the packing of global events, products and frameworks in local contexts, not to de-localise the local, but rather to change its content, not least in terms of identity. An interesting consequence of the connection between local identities and international normative patterns of behaviour, for example, is that they tend to reinforce each other. As we have seen in Indonesia, the state cannot legitimately force ethnic groups into submission by appealing to national security without immediately having the international community respond. This is because having an ethnic identity in addition to a national one is legitimate in the eyes of the international community, as spelled out in the International Convention on the Elimination of All Forms of Discrimination that Indonesia ratified on 25 September 1999 (Castles and Davidson 2000). As a humanitarian approach now forms part of the IMF's humanitarian platform, and the IMF constitutes one of the main designers of Indonesia's previous structural adjustment programme, post-Suharto Indonesian governments have been forced to initiate policies including economic decentralisation and regional autonomy to guarantee the rights of ethnic groups to participate in the current transformation of the Indonesian state and nation. This relates to the organisational, political, ideological and economic aspects of nation building. Ethnic groups thus have, at least theoretically, international support in their jockeying for cultural recognition and political influence.[15]

The international community is gradually becoming more globally encompassing and more deeply entrenched in the individual nation-state. This enlargement of the international space at the expense of the nation-state has created new transnational spaces that are heavily contested by various subnational groups, which utilise them for transnational networking, providing substance to what Maria Montserrat Guibernau, in an article from 1996, has tentatively termed 'nations without states'. Before I turn to those 'in between' spaces or new frameworks for processes of non-statist regionalisation, it is important to address the question of the composition of the state-cum-nation in a global era.

1.7   Towards a disaggregation of nation and state?

Taking the volatile developments within the international community into account, one must ask whether the classical form of the state has reached its climax, historically speaking. For David Jacobson (1998), new transnational, international and regional entities, from international human rights institutions to the EU, are all constraining the state in certain respects and enhancing its role in others. Jacobson argues that today we are witnessing a gradual disaggregation of the nation-state. The political, communal and territorial components of the nation-state, once thought to be deeply entangled, are gradually being unbundled. Territory no longer constitutes identity, as a territory and a people are no longer viewed as inextricably linked. Diasporas and virtual transnational identities are increasingly common. Jacobson stresses, however, that the state is not in decline; on the contrary, its bureaucratic role is enhanced. It is the marriage between state and nation that is in question (Jacobson 1998: 444).

To assess this, I take as a point of departure one of the defining characteristics of the classical concept of the nation-state, namely citizenship. As discussed previously, this was and still is determined in terms of either *ius sanguinis* or *ius soli*. Despite the differences between the two concepts, they both refer to individuals who belong to a coherent entity made up of a functional relationship between state and nation.

One of the main characteristics of the present era, besides those described earlier, is a high degree of labour mobility and migration of various kinds. These movements are closely related to economic globalisation that enforces a complex region-wide distribution of production modes and sites according to where it is most profitable. This encourages higher levels of transnational labour migration, as labour conditions wax and wane according to changing economic tides globally as well as within the individual nation-state. This mobility of people between nations and regions exerts a major pressure on the concept of citizenship to cope with the flow of non-citizens across national borders. Malaysia today is a good case in point, with its high intake of Indonesian and Indian migrant labourers, which periodically causes a political outcry by Malay politicians trying to promote Malay workers. However, ethnic Malays are not inclined to take up the jobs that the Indonesians and Indian workers do, those in construction and menial jobs in the service sector.

Most of these migrants cannot become citizens in Malaysia, as they do not meet the preconditions of either *ius sanguinis* or *ius soli*. Instead, they are categorised as either denizens (foreigners with permanent residence) or margizens (contract workers or undocumented workers) (Schuilenburg 2008). As such, they are marginalised by their community, lacking political influence and access to economic and social benefits.

According to the discussion on the relationship between the international community and the nation-state, the notion of promoting singular nationalities in a globalising world does not make sense in the contemporary processes of regionalisation. However, this does not seem to seep into the diplomatic discourse on statist-initiated regional cooperation. For example, during a seminar series on the relationship between China and ASEAN at Hong Kong University in January 2003, in which diplomats from China presented their views on East and Southeast Asian regionalism, it was repeatedly emphasised that the main building blocks for regional cooperation were first and foremost mutual respect for national sovereignty, non-interference in national affairs and regional cooperation based on consensus, leaving binding treaties out of the question. In relation to regional cooperation per se, the diplomats emphasised that even though it was framed within a multinational forum, the ultimate relationship between the member states was based on non-binding bilateral agreements. The so-called ASEAN Free Trade Area, which is set to eliminate import tariffs by 2015, is in for a difficult period, as it entails a softening stand on current perceptions of national sovereignty.

This official Chinese view of regional cooperation within East and Southeast Asia clashes head on with an analytical approach to the relationship between the international community and nation-states as discussed earlier. China's view is an almost Hobbesian-inspired anarchic perception of the relationship between sovereign states. Perhaps this perception was guided by the nature of the speakers at the seminar as they were all diplomats representing the views of their respective governments.

Nonetheless, the conventional notions of citizenship, *ius sanguinis* and *ius soli*, together with classifications of migrants of various sorts as either denizens or margizens, are increasingly being attacked by a transforming international community, which is forcing individual nation-states to revise their notions of citizenship. This applies especially to those nation-states that base their citizenship on principles of *ius sanguinis,* which includes most of the countries in the Asia Pacific region. As glocalisation increasingly encroaches on the sovereign aspect of nation-hood, thereby facilitating a growing flow of migrant workers across borders, paradoxically these migrants are increasingly confronting problems when settling down in their host communities, as these countries impose new rules to regulate the influx of labour, attempting to tighten national borders. The main question to be addressed in this connection is how long the conventional statist perception of sovereignty and citizenship within a coherent national framework can hold against the changing tides within the international community of which they are an unbreakable part (Ong 1999).

The contradictions between political rhetoric as forwarded by the diplomats concerning the importance of upholding national coherence in relation to statist-initiated regionalisation programmes and actual political and economic societal transformations within, for example, Southeast Asia, are gradually becoming exposed. This is because statist-induced regionalism in the form of political, economic and military cooperation clashes with a deepening transnational fluidity of the social, cultural and political landscape across the region, thus exhibiting a progressive disaggregation between the state and its national hinterland.

To sum up the complex processes behind the notion of glocalisation, Stuart Hall (1997) once wrote that for capital to maintain its global position, it has to incorporate and partly reflect the social and cultural differences it is trying to overcome. He continues:

> Is this the ever-rolling march of the old form of commodification, the old form of globalization, fully in the keeping of capital, fully in the keeping of the West, which is simply able to absorb everybody else within its drive? Or is there something important about the fact that, at a certain point, globalization cannot proceed without learning to live with and working through differences?
>
> (Hall 1997: 30–33)

Ulf Hannerz tried to answer this question by identifying two tendencies in the long-term reconstruction of peripheral cultures within the global *ecumene,* as he called the glocalised community, namely that of saturation and maturation. In relation to saturation, he suggested that as the different transnational manifestations influence peripheral cultures, the latter will step by step assimilate more of the imported meanings and forms, thereby gradually becoming indistinguishable from the centre. What is considered local culture is more or less penetrated by the transnational, which changes it a bit compared to what it was before, although the contrast between the local and the transnational can still be drawn and is still regarded as significant, at least by the local cultures themselves.

> The cultural differences celebrated and recommended for safeguarding now may only be a pale reflection of what once existed, and will sooner or later be gone as well, replaced by other forms of hybridization.
>
> (Hannerz 1997: 122–123)

The tendency of maturation reflects processes of recontextualisations of global influences into a localised frame of understanding to use them in local sociopolitical discourses. Ulf Hannerz wrote that culturally defined frameworks of life also possess the power to colonise the market framework. The periphery takes its time reshaping metropolitan culture to its own specifications. It is in this phase that the metropolitan forms in the periphery are most marked by their purity, but on closer scrutiny they are ineffective and vulnerable in their relative isolation. In phase two, and in innumerable phases thereafter, as they are made to interact with whatever else exists in their new setting, the metropolitan forms are no longer so easily recognisable; they themselves have become hybridised. Local entrepreneurs have gradually learned to master the alien cultural forms, which reach them through the transnational commodity flow, to such a degree that the resulting new forms are more responsive to, and in part outgrowths of, local everyday life (Hannerz 1997: 123–124).

1.8 Ethnicity and sustainability of the nation-state

Taking my point of departure in the glocal exchange of culture and identities as delineated by Hall and Hannerz, I agree with Rita Smith Kipp, who defined ethnicity as something that cannot be determined by simply noting the differences between people. Instead, one has to concentrate on which differences matter to people and how these differences become culturally embedded (Kipp 1993: 17–24). Employing this broad definition of ethnic identity, I furthermore concur with Benedict Anderson that the politics of ethnicity has its roots in modern times, not ancient history, regardless of how ethnicities are ideologised (Anderson 1987: 10).

Ethnicity, then, can be conceived of as an imaginative framework that encompasses a variety of related identities. These identities are understood as products of ascription and self-ascription, and are generally based on ideologies of common descent. Following Katherine Verdery (1994), ethnicity furthermore can be conceived of as constituting a cultural matrix for a given social organisation. The point of departure for analysing ethnicity, according to Verdery and others, is thus not culture per se, but rather the potential aspect of social or political manipulation of identities and thus their 'situational' character (Verdery 1994: 34–35; see also Barth 1994: 12–13). The cultural matrix then, besides being an important aspect of the local socialisation process, constitutes a reservoir of identity markers that a given social organisation relates to when expressing itself in terms of ethnicity.

Linking ethnicity to social organisation makes it contemporary, not primordial, meaning that an ethnic identity is not based on some 'objective' cultural features. Ethnicity and affiliated identities are thus situational and fluid in content and as such very politically potent. Fredric Barth wrote that leaders who pursue their own political agenda affect the mobilisation of ethnic groups in collective action and as such do not necessarily express their groups' cultural ideologies or represent a popular will (Barth 1994: 12–13). I concur with this and will maintain that a revival of cultural identity can also be interpreted as local aspirations to (re-)create a political community.

Because of the fluidity and thus the political potential of ethnicity, many states perceive ethnic groups as a threat to national unity (Brown 1994: 2). Depending on the organisation of the state, its ideology can be made to accommodate the various alternative identities found within the national territory. For example, the Indonesian national motto, '*Bhinneka Tunggal Ika*' or 'Unity in Diversity' is a case in point. This is in recognition of the state's limited ability to control the development of ethnic identities and the resilience of ethnic groups to attempts to transform or contain them. What is not up for discussion, however, is the state's perception of having the exclusive or sovereign right to manipulate those ideologies and to enforce its interpretation with power if need be. In this sense, the claim to sovereignty is of utmost importance for the state.

Institutions such as the IMF, WTO, ILO and the UN have a history of intervening in national political and economic policies, especially in times of crisis. Paradoxically, these international forces empower, so to speak, the various ethnic and religious groups, thereby enabling them to mount pressure on the state to grant them political autonomy and cultural recognition (Smith 1990; Brown 1995: 54–68; Friedman 1998: 1–19). The process of empowerment has in many cases in Southeast Asia led to the creation of resistance movements that have tried to mobilise 'the people' in order to further their claims. Various Muslim groups in Malaysia, Indonesia and in the southern part of the Philippines are cases in point. For example, in Indonesia we have seen the revival of a whole range of ethnic and religious groups, which have become more vocal after the collapse of the New Order regime in May 1998. The empowerment of these groups has not created secessionist movements. Instead they are concerned with cultural recognition and political positioning in post-Suharto Indonesia (Jakobsen 1999).

At times the relationship between state and nation is tense, the nation identified as a constellation of ethnic groups jockeying for cultural recognition and political power, thus pressuring the state to react to this internal political dynamic to maintain its control and legitimacy over the nation. At the same time, the international community is also squeezing the state to allow ethnic groups to exercise their rights as spelled out in various international charters; the state finds itself squeezed on both sides of the global and local context. When developing economic plans for the further development of the nation-state, it has to serve two masters: its own citizens and the global community, including the global economic community, as the state needs to attract foreign direct investment to legitimate its policies towards civil society. By employing the term *glocalisation* for the complexity within the triangular matrix as outlined earlier, it is possible to trace the various connections between the global, national and subnational levels.

After having outlined four different approaches to understand the global economy, it has become clear that for the present purpose, the glocalised approach is the best suited for this study, as it integrates the various kinds of dynamic forces at the global, national and local levels at the same time and shows how the three are intimately related. The first approach discussed in this chapter dealt with whether it is possible to decouple from the global economy. It then moved on to the second approach, which discussed whether the global economy is 'spiky' or 'flat'. This led to the third approach that divided the global economy into different types of markets to be able to identify the different forces at play there. All three approaches had the same tendency to disregard the ability of the national as well as the local level to impact the functionality of the global economy, thus portraying the global economy as a kind of juggernaut forcing both the national and local levels into compliance with global demands. These three approaches constitute a top-down approach when studying the workings of global economics and how it impacts national and local levels. The fourth approach, a glocalised approach, studies the impact of the global economy on a triangular matrix consisting of global political and economic developments, the role of the state and the civil society and how these three points in the triangle impact and relate to each other.

By combining the perspectives of all three points in the triangle it is clear how the different levels of analysis are permeated by strong ties of interdependency and integration. According to this approach, it is not possible to decouple from the global economy, to provide a kind of '*still-leben*' in terms of spikes, hills and valleys, nor to divide it into different types of markets. It is only an approach based on a glocalised perspective that is capable of identifying the strings of interdependency and integration, and then delineating the delicate web that exists between the different levels that determine the functionality between the global and the local. This approach will be applied in the following chapters to Malaysia, and in particular Penang, to account for the present state of the global and local in this particular context. Malaysia and Penang thus constitute a test case for the application of this particular approach based on a glocal perspective. Before doing that, however, it is important to take yet another look at international business theory as specific aspects of this school of thought provide the background for the theoretical approach to analyse Malaysia and Penang respectively in accordance with a glocalised perspective.

Notes

1 www.cia.gov/library/publications/the-world-factbook/fields/2003.html. Accessed on 9 October 2012.
2 For a more detailed discussion in this connection, see Gesteland (2005) and Nisbeth *et al.* (2001).
3 Conrad de Aenlle, 'Decoupling: Theory vs. Reality', *The New York Times,* 7 February 2008.
4 Ibid.
5 Friedman's ten flatteners are: harmonisation and integration, pushed forward by the collapse of the Berlin Wall, Netscape, workflow software, outsourcing, offshoring, uploading, supply chaining, insourcing and in-forming.
6 Defined as wireless, voice over Internet and file sharing.
7 Defined as the convergence of the ten 'flatteners', horizontalisation of business practices and economic liberalisation of emerging markets.
8 For a more detailed discussion of the role of institutions in various types of markets, see North (1991), Scott (2008).

9 For a full discussion of LMEs and CMEs, see Stephenson (2002).

10 For a further reading on varieties of capitalism, see Whitley (1998), Hall and Soskice (2001) and Carney *et al.* (2009).

11 For a further discussion of the notion of trust, see Fukuyama (1995).

12 For a pertinent case study in this connection see 'Realities of Emerging Markets: Some Lessons from Unilever's Strategy for Lifebuoy & Sunsilk in India' (www.icmrindia. org/casestudies/catalogue/Marketing1/MKTA008.htm) (*Case Studies Collection*) (2008).

13 www.fanmilk.com/index.php?id=85. Accessed on 17 September 2013.

14 For a case study on glocalisation, see Jain *et al.* 2012.

15 For a general discussion of the relationship between minority rights, national sovereignty and the international human rights regime, see Castles and Davidson (2000: 208–212).

2 Employing an international business approach when studying the triangular matrix of glocalisation

After having delineated various approaches to the study of the global economy and settled on glocalisation as the main theoretical approach to read the global economy, this chapter will refine the theoretical lens on which the triangular matrix on glocalisation is based, especially the part that focuses on how the global economy impacts a national economy. This will be done using an international business (IB) approach to analyse a national economy, in this case the Malaysian economy. This will not be done according to the normal procedure in IB studies, using a market-based analysis, but rather on the basis of a glocalised approach to the study of the relationship between the global economy and a national economy and the ramifications of this on a given societal landscape. In other words, IB theories are not to be employed exclusively in an economic sphere, but are to relate to a variety of societal factors that have a positive or negative impact on the explanatory power of the individual IB theories employed.

This approach positions those theories in a critical perspective, as the individual theories are exposed to a context that puts a strain on their employability and explanatory capabilities. Because of this, various IB theories will be combined into a model in which the individual theory is supported by one or more related IB theories that can constitute either a specific theoretical model designed exclusively for, for example, the Malaysian case or a generic model that can be employed on other national economies. In the context of this book, the IB models are specifically designed to fit the Malaysian economy, but elements of the model can be developed into a more generic one without major difficulties.

To give an idea of how such a model can be designed, several interrelated IB theories have been combined (Figure 2.1).

The selection of IB theories in Figure 2.1 can be combined into one major model or into several smaller ones. The size and composition depends on the context in which the model is to be applied. Overall, the context is a national economy in an emerging market. The point of departure for the model is Dunning's (2000) Elective Paradigm, the so-called OLI model. Basically, the model depicts a company that has decided to go international. To assess whether the company's ownership-specific advantages ('O') can be maintained during an internationalisation process Barney's (1991) Resource Based View (RBV) is applied. After having checked whether the tangible and intangible company resources are applicable in a specific

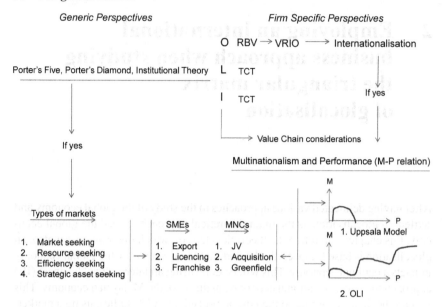

Figure 2.1 IBS in a 'glocalised' economy

Source: Own design July 2012

foreign market, a further check on the ownership-specific advantages is carried out by employing the so-called VRIO framework, also developed by Barney, in 2001. VRIO stands for: value creation (V), rarity (R), limitability (I) and organisation (O).[1] An affirmative answer to each question indicates that a firm can sustain a competitive advantage in, for example, a foreign market.

If both the RBV and the VRIO sanction the initiation of an internationalisation process, the company theoretically has two new options to operationalise the internationalisation procedure, namely an incremental approach using the Uppsala model or a 'head on' approach, that is, entering a foreign market that is not closely linked to the company's home market by employing the OLI model. To give an example of the latter approach, a Danish company goes directly to a pertinent Asian market without first accumulating experiences in either Scandinavian or European markets. As a consequence, the company confronts a rather steep learning curve that is more or less dictated by a trial and error approach.[2] Depending on the size of the company, an appropriate entry mode can now be selected. For SMEs, the options most often employed are exporting, licensing or franchising because of budget constraints; in the case of a larger company, options revolve around joint ventures (JV), partial and full acquisitions or various types of greenfield investments. This list of entry modes is not exhaustive; these are just the most typical ones employed.

If we now turn to the location-specific advantages ('L') in the OLI model, the perspective turns from employing firm-specific theories to generic ones. After a company first assesses location-specific advantages to see whether the market in question is positive towards its products and/or services, it then checks whether the company's specific resources and capabilities, as determined through the RBV and VRIO, can be sustained in a particular market. If so, the company proceeds by employing more generic theories such as institutional theory as defined by North (1991) and Scott (1995) when positioning the targeted foreign market in an overall societal context.[3] These theoretical insights into the relationship between formal and informal institutions in a given societal context and how they in return react to and impact international business provide companies with an analytical and dynamic understanding of how the market they are interested in works. This is important as such knowledge has a major impact on which business strategy as well as which entry mode to employ when entering that particular market.

After carrying out this generic macro-analysis, our company is interested in becoming more familiar with the competitive environment in a pertinent domestic industry in which the company is to engage. Here Porter's Five Forces or his Diamond models (1990, 2008) can be employed, depending on whether the state is an active and perhaps a dominant player in that particular market or just to assess in what way the state tries to facilitate the industry in question. If our fictitious company is satisfied with the market and the industry analysis, it is now, according to our model, ready to make the final identification of what kind of market it is seeking and thus what kind of entry mode to employ. The selection made using the generic-market analysis should match the selection made on the basis of the firm-specific analysis. If this is the case, then the company is almost ready to enter the foreign market, relatively sure of making the best of the opportunities and constraints awaiting it there.

There is, however, according to Dunning (2000), one final analysis to make, namely an analysis of the internalisation advantages, the so-called I factor. According to Peng and Meyer (2011: 173–174), when focusing on the 'I', one is focusing on how to organise the value chain. This means, how to organise company assets and potential suppliers and subcontractors, thus deciding on whether the value chain should be organised 'in house' or whether the new market can be drawn on in sourcing the supplies necessary for the company to succeed in this market. One of the key considerations in this connection is transaction costs. If our company can replace local market suppliers it will do so, because of the fact that the transaction cost is lower than if it sources what it needs from local suppliers. The tendency to internalise and thus tighten up the value chain becomes much stronger when the foreign market is characterised by market failures. Basically this means that the imperfections that characterise the foreign market mechanism make some of the transaction costs prohibitively high for our company. Thus, it will choose to tighten up the value chain, that is, internalise the production process to the highest degree possible to keep down the cost of doing business in that market.

If we now return to the overall IB model shown in Figure 2.1, we can see that the OLI paradigm constitutes the main point of departure for employing both a firm-specific perspective and a more generic-market perspective of a given company's internationalisation strategy. As such, the overall model provides some basic input for developing a business strategy designed to deal with both the positive and negative outcomes of the firm-specific and generic-market perspectives. This again constitutes the basis for selecting what entry mode to employ in a particular market. In this way, the business strategy that takes its point of departure in part from a business model and in part from the outcome of both the firm-specific and generic perspective analyses of the market is thus attuned to the local institutional arrangement, both the formal and informal, as well as dealing with the specificities of the local market in the most optimal way. Our company is now amply prepared to initiate its internationalisation process.

2.1   Societal embeddedness in economic approaches

The overall model or any combination of it works most efficiently under perfect market conditions, at least theoretically. Perfect competition serves as a benchmark against which to measure real-life and imperfectly competitive markets. The assumption of perfect market competition as the foundation of price theory for product markets is often criticised for making agents passive, that is, removing active attempts to increase one's welfare or profits by price undercutting, product design, advertising or innovation, activities that critics argue characterise most industries and markets. This criticism is reinforced when comparing the three modes of reading the global economy, which are, regardless of which perception you prefer, socially and politically sanitised versions of how the markets work. In other words, they are ideal modes of reading the global economy.

For example, if we take the three descriptions of the global economy discussed in the previous chapter – integration versus decoupling, whether the global economy is flat or spiky, and the IB approach that operates on the basis of market differentiation – all three operate with a rather standardised notion of international business practices in which the societal embeddedness of the global economy does not have a significant impact on economic performance, internationally or domestically. The same lack of impact from societal forces on state performance in the three perspectives also applies to the main non-economic player in this context, namely the role of the state, regardless of whether it acts as an initiator of economic activity or as a facilitator in both the national and global economies.

The option of decoupling is measured against the political possibility of withdrawing or at least shielding the national economy from the impact of the global economy, and whether the global economy is flat or spiky depends on how the economy is organised on both a global and national level. The societal impact on the economy, whichever level, is strongly underplayed, thus basing economic performance on almost perfect market conditions. The fourth and final approach to seeing the global economy was identified as a glocalised perception of both the global and national economies. This approach strongly indicates that societal factors have a major impact on the performance and functionality of the economy, both the global and national, as well as on state performance. The main premise here is that (societal) contexts matter when working on economic developments regardless of level, and on the functionality of the state, regardless of type. Because of the inclusive or holistic perception on which glocalisation is based, it is the one preferred in this study. There is, however, a weak spot in this connection that has to be taken into account.

2.2 Zooming in on institutional theory

What is actually meant by 'societal context' here? To explain this, I will focus in particular on institutional theory, as this approach constitutes the background knowledge against which more firm-specific theories within IB theories are positioned. It is also the approach where analysts benefit the most when measuring the impact of societal embeddedness on economic performance. The key elements within institutional theory are the relationships between various kinds of institutions. According to Scott,

> institutions are social structures that have attained a high degree of resilience. They are composed of cultural-cognitive, normative, and regulative elements that, together with associated activities and resources, provide stability and meaning to social life. Institutions are transmitted by various types of carriers, including symbolic systems, relational systems, routines, and artefacts. Institutions operate at different levels of jurisdiction, from the world system to localized interpersonal relationships. Institutions by definition connote stability but are subject to change processes, both incremental and discontinuous.
>
> (Scott 1995: 33)[4]

Scott's sociological approach to institutions and their embeddedness and dynamics within a given societal context is quite intriguing and revealing, but it does not contain the specific international business angle to institutions that I am looking for. Douglass North's 1991 article on institutions summarises much of his earlier work on economic and institutional change. Here North defines institutions as 'humanly devised constraints that structure political, economic and social interactions' (North 1991: 97). Constraints, as North describes, are devised as formal rules (constitutions, laws, property rights, etc.) and informal restraints (sanctions, taboos, customs, traditions, code of conduct, etc.), which usually contribute to the perpetuation of order and safety within a market or society. The degree to which they are effective is subject to varying circumstances, such as a government's limited coercive force, a lack of an organised state, or the presence of strong religious precepts (North 1991: 97–112).

At a first glance this more economically oriented approach to the role of institutions in a societal context provides us with a more direct understanding of how institutions, societal factors in general and business relate to each other in a rather operational manner. To set in motion the dynamic relationship between the three nodes mentioned earlier, the market differentiation that IB theories is based on and relates to comes in handy. As mentioned in the previous chapter, according to IB theories, markets can be divided into three main types: developed markets, emerging markets and bottom-of-the-pyramid markets. The difference between these three main types is the way the formal and informal institutions relate to each other. On the basis of this, the following market characteristics can be identified.

Developed markets. These markets are characterised by firmly implemented institutions that are backed by law, thus keeping modifying and potentially desta-bilising forces from the informal institutions at bay. This kind of market and the accompanying societal institutional arrangements are characterised as 'high-trust' societies by Fukuyama (1995), as individuals have confidence in the overall soci-etal organisation and believe in the implementation, functionality and impartiality of the formal institutions.

Emerging and transitional markets. These markets are generally defined as hav-ing more or less functioning formal rules and regulations. The informal institutions are characterised by traditional norms and religious practices combined with col-lectivist and family-oriented value systems. These informal institutions have a great impact on the implementation and functionality of the formal institutions, thus necessitating the development of strong business-to-business networks (B2B) as well as strong business-to-government networks (B2G) to deal with institutional voids. Furthermore, some of these markets are in the process of moving from a planned economy to an open market economy. The most obvious examples here are Russia, the Eastern European countries, India, China and Vietnam. They can furthermore be characterised as having high growth rates and very competitive, low-cost production. They are high-risk economies with unstable political regimes. In general, the societies in this category of markets can be defined as low-trust societies, as individuals generally do not trust the formal institutions because of heavy influence from informal institutions.

BOP markets. These markets are characterised by an almost complete absence of formal institutions. This means that informal institutions in the form of kinship relations, religious communities and localised norms and values are the governing features in this kind of market. Seen from a business perspective, access to this market is not through high profit margins but through high volume and low profit margins, as the purchasing power of potential consumers is around less than US$4 a day (Peng 2009: 6). The main companies working in these markets are often successful first movers. Two examples of these are Unilever Hindustan and Fan Milk International, as mentioned in Chapter 1.

2.3   Informal institutions: the 'black hole' in institutional theory?

Moving beyond a simple application of institutional theory on a given type of market and returning to a more general discussion of the theory per se, it is possible to argue that North's perception of the relationships between formal and informal institutions represents a rather circular and functionalist explanation. I base this assumption on that they, that is, the formal and informal institutions, according to North, condition each other. This means that the implementation and functionality of the formal insti-tutions depend to a large extent on the impact from the informal institutions (North 1991: 97). I argue that such a functionalist reading of the relationship between the two does not necessarily exist. It could just as well be that informal institutional constraints simply block the development, implementation and functionality of the formal institutions, thus increasing the scope of the so-called institutional voids, also defined as the absence of intermediaries that facilitate the functioning of the market (Khanna *et al.* 2005). We are thus not talking about a mutual dependent relationship between the two but rather an unpredictable and conflicting impact on behalf of the informal institutions on the formal ones.

If we now take a closer look at what Scott (2010) has to say about institutions, both formal and informal ones, the following interesting observation about the relationship between the two is relevant for this study. As mentioned earlier:

> Institutions are social structures that have attained a high degree of resilience and are composed of *cultural-cognitive, normative* and *regulative elements* that together with associated activities and resources provide stability and meaning to social life.
>
> (Scott 2010: 6)

In order to move beyond a mere listing of these three institutional characteristics, I suggest that we 'read' them from the perspective of how we store experiences in the form of expanding our meta-cognitive capabilities so as to navigate in the most sensible and strategic way those cultural-cognitive, normative and regulative elements that normally characterise informal institutions. The idea behind this suggestion is to link these characteristics to individuals who basically constitute the agents that man and impute dynamics into what kind of institutions we are talking about. As a kind of following up on this, I suggest that we look further into how we handle the experience of unfamiliarity, how we navigate an unfamiliar social landscape, how the experience of this learning process adds to our meta-cognitive capabilities, and finally how we label the unfamiliar as 'culture', either as our own or a culture that belongs to the 'other', the strangers. Posing these kind of questions allows us to venture further into the current 'black hole' that informal institutions constitute. To follow up on this let us take a closer look at each of the three elements. Scott writes:

> Those stressing *regulative elements* give more attention to rational choice and design. Regulative elements are more formalized, more explicit, more easily planned and strategically manipulated.
>
> (2010: 6)

Here Scott is talking about formal institutions that guide and/or structure social behaviour. Informal institutions are to some extent suppressed in order to conform to formal requirements. He continues:

> Scholars emphasizing *normative elements* stress the social embeddedness of political and economic behaviour.
>
> (2010: 6, cited in Granovetter 1985)

Normative elements are more difficult to identify, as they can be found in both formal and informal institutions. If normative elements, for example, originate from within the informal institutional setup, that is, from various cultural specific groupings within the national hinterland, then these cultural specific normative elements have the capability to impact the functionality of the formal institutions because of the fact that representatives from these cultural-specific groups are employed in the various formal institutions. Because of this the latter might work in multiple ways not envisioned by the formal requirements that define their functionality in the first place. The reason for this is that actors migrate between formal and informal institutions, normatively colouring them in the process according to their personal (meta-cognitive) and social (cultural) backgrounds.

If the normative elements emanate from the regulative elements, then we are talking about imposing official norms of behaviour in, say, a multicultural national landscape. We thus have normative elements that flow back and forth between the formal and informal institutions as well as within the formal and informal institutions respectively. This is an important observation when trying to identify key markers that actors create to help them navigate an unfamiliar social or administrative landscape.

As a kind of these suppositions Scott goes on to say:

> Personal ties and informal relations with co-workers, as well as specific situational demands, often trump narrowly defined self-interest and utilitarian concerns.
>
> (2010: 6)

Here he almost negates the notion of rational choice and designs previously stressed that define the regulative elements, thus emphasising context and situatedness as key signifiers in social interaction. This leads us to the third and final group of elements, namely the *cultural-cognitive elements*. Elaborating on this, Scott says:

> The most recent contributors to the institutional discourse are those scholars who stress the importance of cultural-cognitive elements. *The elements are cultural* because they are socially constructed symbolic representations; *they are cognitive* in that they provide vital templates for framing individual perceptions and decisions.
>
> (2010: 7)

Before commenting on this, I would like to cite Scott once more:

> Cultural-cognitive elements provide the bedrock for normative prescriptions and regulative controls, because norms and rules must refer to institutionally constituted entities. However, they are also capable by themselves of providing a framework for order. . . . Although these three elements exert an independent effect on social order and it is possible to identify situations in which one or another is predominant, they most often appear in varying combinations to

collectively undergird existing social arrangements. But even in such situations, differences among the three elements give rise to dilemmas and tensions, sparking misunderstandings, conflicts and confusion that open up possibilities for change.

(2010: 7)

According to his final comment on the relationship between the three elements, he perceives them as constituting a total societal entity, as inter-dependent elements that together form the overall framework for what happens within a society. Arguably, this is somewhat problematic as I see the different societies in Southeast Asia, and in this particular case Malaysia, as consisting of several societies within an overall national society, framed in an ethnically defined hierarchical or stratified order. This means that dividing Malaysia into one set of formal and informal institutions is a simplified way of seeing this society. There are several societies within the Malaysian society that coexist, not in a symmetrical societal structure but rather in a layered and politically engineered order (the ethnic Malays at the top, the ethnic Chinese in the middle and the ethnic Indians at the bottom of the societal pyramid). The social landscape in which, for example, Malaysian ethnic Chinese entrepreneurs are to navigate is thus not a one-dimensional landscape but a multi-layered one that consists of a complex multi-ethnic web of normative prescriptions that is not always easy to disentangle for a given actor. This is complicated by the Malaysian government's politically engineered management of that complexity.[5]

Arguably, the overall framework for navigating this landscape consists of different sets of regulative, normative and cultural-cognitive elements that together make up the Malaysian nation. Thus when an ethnic Chinese entrepreneur is to navigate that part of the societal landscape that he knows the best, he cannot only focus on his local bit of it, but has to take the overall cultural-cognitive elements into account, as they too constitute parts of the socially constructed symbolic representations of his own immediate landscape. This complex social landscape constitutes the background against which he is to identify the different societal 'markets' and then navigate them. We are thus talking about informal institutions within informal institutions as identified by Scott. From a strategic point of view, the ethnic Chinese entrepreneur will navigate only those aspects of the overall informal institutions that are of relevance for him here and now. For him the keyword is thus *context*.

This reading of Scott's three constituent institutional elements fits perfectly into a perception of a multi-layered national ethnic landscape. The point of departure here is thus not only the local ethnically distinct markers that our entrepreneur tries to identify in his immediate social landscape but first and foremost a meta-cognitive understanding of the overall national multi-ethnic landscape; only after that can he identify those markers that he intends to use to navigate in his immediate surroundings. We are still talking about social constructs, that is, the markers, which have their origins in the meta-cognitive repertoire of a given navigator. They are originally thus not loaded with a given cultural bias. They only become 'cultural' when our entrepreneur experiences them as unfamiliar in relation to his meta-cognitive and/or tacit pool of experience.

To further zoom in on how to specify the dynamics governing the various informal institutions, I suggest employing a twofold analytical approach consisting of an etic and an emic perspective so as to capture the diffuse nature of these institutions.

An etic perspective is similar to the typical way we work with IB theories, that is, from an investor perspective looking at a given market. Basically it is to assess a given market, be it a developed, an emerging or a BOP market. This perception of etic was originally coined by the linguist Kenneth L. Pike in 1967.[6] His definition is still widely used in anthropological studies. He defines an etic account as a description of a norm or belief formulated by an observer that is external to the culture studied (see also Keesing 1976). Put simply, this means, ideally speaking, that an etic account attempts to be culturally neutral, as it is foreign to the observer's own cultural background.[7]

A general definition of an emic perspective goes beyond the etic observations and focuses on how local investors and entrepreneurs perceive, navigate and/or handle the informal constraints (and of course also formal institutions). This definition is also in accordance with Pike's definition of emic, namely that an emic account is a description of behaviour or beliefs that are meaningful (consciously or unconsciously) to the actor; that is, an emic account comes from a person who originates from the culture under investigation. Most accounts that are recorded directly from an indigenous informant contribute to building up an emic perspective.

Combining etic and emic perspectives on informal institutional constraints not only provides us with another and perhaps complementary empirical set of data compared to an account based purely on an etic account, but also includes data emanating from local entrepreneurs and other pertinent indigenous informants. This provides us with a holistic perspective of how to perceive informal institutional constraints and how they impact formal ones, setting the scene for a qualified analysis of the global-local nexus, thereby disclosing the interconnectedness between the economic, political and societal aspects on which this book is based, namely a glocalised approach.

2.4   A note on culture in international business literature

So far the notion of culture both in a generic form and in relation to international business has not been mentioned. This does not mean that this concept is not important in this context. The reason why I first deal with the notion of culture at this stage is that I would like to question the use of culture as an explanatory concept or framework of the aforementioned definitions of informal institutions. The use of culture in international business literature abounds and confuses more than clarifies because of the fact that it is poorly defined, if at all. There are national cultures, organisational cultures and societal cultures, just to mention the concepts most often referred to. The following is an attempt to clarify why the notion of culture in business studies is problematic and what other explanations can be forwarded, thus avoiding the 'veil of mist' in which the use of culture generally clouds these studies. First, I will discuss different uses of culture in international business studies. Then I will move on to show that the analysis or use of 'culture' in a business context is not the same as an anthropological notion of culture. As it is used in contemporary international business literature, the term *culture* covers social and societal processes that on the surface produce images of what we normally identify as culture, whether in a national, organisational or societal context.

For example, according to Hofstede (1991), national cultural values differ mainly along four (later five) dimensions identified as: power distance, individualism/ collectivism, masculinity/femininity, uncertainty avoidance and finally Confucian values. These dimensions and values constitute a framework that can be used to compare countries quantitatively and assess differences in national cultures. Hofstede characterises culture as a sum of values, customs and beliefs that collectively programme an individual's mind, thus making them believe that they form part of an imagined community.

Hofstede's notion of culture and his five dimensions are rather problematic. The data on which his study are based originates from fieldwork that he conducted among IBM employees from more than seventy countries during the period 1967 to 1973. The data are generally perceived as outdated and static, as no follow-up study has been undertaken and thus they represent a snapshot of this particular period in time. Therefore, they do not take into account that huge changes have occurred in the economy, market and society after this period.

Fang goes against this static notion of culture and suggests that the nature of culture is dialectical and paradoxical and that one should embrace such opposite forces instead of thinking that everything must be 'either/or' (Fang 2006: 72–73). He compares culture to the ocean. The wave patterns of the ocean symbolise the visible values and behaviours. There is, however, more depth to the ocean than merely the waves on the surface. This means that there is more depth to culture than the behaviours that are on the surface. Furthermore, there are numerous ebbs and flows underneath the surface where unknown cultural values and behaviours are. Given internal yin-yang-like mechanisms, that is, societal forces that balance out each other, and external forces, such as economic and political globalisation, these unknown values might surface to become the visible and guiding values and patterns at the next historical moment. Fang incorporates the ocean and yin-yang metaphors to emphasise that neither national nor organisational culture is static but rather dynamic and has the ability to change and adapt to local specificities, depending on time and context.

Basically Fang's ocean metaphor claims that culture changes and the modern individual is not constrained by cultural beliefs but adapts to changes in the societal make-up (Fang 2006: 83–85). In a sense, Fang's blue ocean perception of culture relates closely to Yoshikawa's dialogical model on how to handle the crossing of cultural boundaries. According to Yoshikawa, individuals do not live isolated from each other. Human beings are only complete when engaging in social relationships; they are thus inevitably interdependent in their very being (Yoshikawa 1987; see also Chen 2002).

Regardless of whether one perceives culture as static or dynamic, one is still employing the notion of culture as a more or less objective construct that provides guidelines for how individuals assess the behaviour of the 'other' and act accordingly. In order to move beyond such an objectified understanding of culture, the focus had to be turned towards those actors who construct and operationalise such notions of 'culture'. One of the scholars who have tried this is Clifford Geertz:

> The concept of culture . . . is essentially a semiotic one. Believing, with Max Weber, that man is an animal suspended in webs of significance he himself has spun, I take culture to be those webs, and the analysis of it to be therefore not an experimental science in search of a law but an interpretive one in search of meaning.
>
> (Geertz 1973: 5)

It is the reference to a semiotic understanding of culture in this quote that I found most conducive for my research on excavating dynamic factors within and among informal institutions in a given societal arrangement. The bridge between the concepts of culture discussed earlier (Hofstede, Fang and Yoshikawa) and a semiotic understanding of culture can be found in Schein's analysis of organisational culture. Schein identifies three distinct levels in organisational cultures: artefacts and behaviours, espoused values and basic assumptions. The three levels refer to the degree to which the different cultural phenomena are visible to the observer. Artefacts include any tangible, overt or verbally identifiable elements in an organisation. Architecture, furniture, dress code and office jokes all exemplify organisational artefacts. Artefacts constitute the visible elements in a culture and they can be recognised by people not part of the culture.

Espoused values are the organisation's stated values and rules of behaviour. Basically these relate to how the members represent the organisation, both to themselves and to others. They are often expressed in official philosophies and public statements of identity. Espoused values can sometimes be a projection for the future, of what the members hope to become. A good example is the mission and vision statements on which a company is based. Another example of this could be codes of employee professionalism, or a 'family first' mantra.

Shared basic assumptions are the deeply embedded, taken-for-granted behaviours, which are usually unconscious, but constitute the essence of an organisational culture. These assumptions are typically so well integrated into the office dynamic that they are hard to recognise from within. They generally originate with the founder(s) of the company and thus constitute the identity of the company (Schein 1985).

Schein's model mainly refers to various normative levels within an organisation or company and how they relate to each other. It could be inferred from this that the model is based on a *tabula rasa* understanding of organisational culture, meaning that employees dispose of their societal normative understanding of how to behave outside the company in which they are employed. It is understood as the normative standard for acceptable conduct and the work ethic while in the company, and that they have to adhere to that particular company culture only as long as they are there. The problem with Schein's model, however, is that it is confined to the company and thus does not link up to the society of which it is a part.

Brannen also takes Schein's model as a point of departure and uses it both as a diagnostic tool to uncover the basic assumption of an organisation and as a comparative tool to heighten organisational cultural differences that matter when managing cross-cultures behaviour (Brannen 2005). However, she goes beyond the confinement mentioned earlier and relates the model to a more generic understanding of the relationship between a company's understanding of 'culture' and the society in which it is embedded. She thus employs a slightly different interpretation of Schein's model, based on artefacts, values and assumptions. Artefacts are on the surface, what can be sensed easily. Values are what can be inferred or articulated. And assumptions are hidden; they can deal with people and the environment, human nature, human roles and relationships, reality, time, risk taking and so forth.

When comparing Brannen to Schein's three levels, it seems as if Brannen is merging organisational and societal normative behaviour, thereby negating the *tabula rasa* in Schein. This is especially true when comparing Schein's 'basic assumptions' and Brannen's 'assumptions'. Whereas Schein exclusively refers to an organisation, Brannen refers to a generic, more societal-related understanding of 'assumptions'.

Taking a point of departure in this difference, the way is now open for a semiotic understanding of cross-cultural differences, or perhaps more correctly, for a semiotic understanding of differences, not only within an organisation but also in a societal context. By focusing on the semiotics of differences one is moving away from focusing on artefacts and values and concentrating instead on the relation between signs and the things or meaning to which they refer.[8] In this way Brannen and Geertz refer to the same thing when Geertz, wrote, as quoted earlier, '*Believing that man is an animal suspended in webs of significance he himself has spun, I take culture to be those webs*'. In a sense, this mode of understanding (cultural) differences negates the notion of culture per se, as it refers to a whole range of social processes that, because of their complexity, obstruct clear-cut explanations of why human beings behave differently in different contexts. By branding these complex processes 'culture', we all know what is referred to! As an illustration of these processes this author has developed a model that indicates the potential problems of not understanding differences in a foreign context (see Figure 2.2).

What is to be noted in this model is the sender's encoding of a message and the receiver's decoding of sender's encoded message might not be the same. The more the sender's social and/or societal context or background differs from the context or background of the receiver's, the greater the chances are of the latter to misinterpret the former's message. The result of such miscommunication is a re-contextualisation of the sender's original message, thus producing a complication in terms of understanding what is being conveyed between the sender and receiver. This is, I believe, where the so-called cultural differences in the form of cultural stereotyping originate. As one thus does not understand the messaged conveyed, then stereotypical perceptions of the 'other' takes over, producing 'real' differences between the sender and receiver. Cultural differences do not arise because of what can be observed or inferred but rather because the semiotic background between

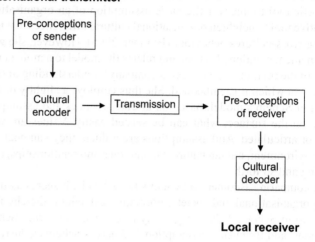

Figure 2.2 Code switching within cross-cultural communication

the parties are different due to differences in normative values and socialisation systems governing the respective societal backgrounds.

These way of thinking about 'cultural' differences permeates the notion of differences in this book. In the chapters to follow, the Chinese entrepreneurs in Penang, Malaysia, are not only classifying themselves as being Chinese due to the fact that their ancestral relations relate them to China. It is also as a result of the discourse of what 'Malay-ness' – understood as a cross-ethnic construct encompassing all the three main ethnic groups in Malaysia, namely the ethnic Malays, ethnic Chinese and ethnic Indians – means and on whose conditions the discourse is based. I shall return to this in greater details in Chapter 4 and in particular in Chapter 5. As for now, it is enough to say that the discourse generally promoted in international business literature by Hofstede 1984, Nisbeth *et al.* 2001 and Gesteland 2005 is based on etic stereotypical understandings of local differences and not on the underlying currents of more or less recontextualised notions of what ethnic identity means. In the following I intend to debunk such stereotypical notions of Chinese-ness by first positioning Malaysia in a Southeast Asian context. We then move on to discuss the origin of the Chinese in the region and then take a closer look at the politically motivated and engineered understanding of ethnicity in a Malaysian societal context. Only then can we understand how Malaysian Chinese-owned SMEs in the automation sector in Penang position themselves, not only in an economic sense but also in a national political sense, a sense that conditions the overall business community per se.

Notes

1 For a detailed discussion of the VRIO framework, see Peng and Meyer (2011, p. 106ff).
2 For a discussion of the Uppsala Model and the OLI paradigm, see Dunning and Lundan (2009), and Johanson and Vahlne (2009).

3 For a detailed discussion of institutional theory, see Peng and Meyer (2011: 35–88).
4 See also Scott (2008, 2010) concerning the study of institutions.
5 For a more detailed description of this ethnic layering and the complex social and political management of it, see Chapter 3.
6 See James Lett on Pike's notion of emic and etic: http://faculty.irsc.edu/faculty/jlett/Article%20on%20Emics%20and%20Etics.htm. Accessed 23 October 2012.
7 For typical examples of etic observations see Nisbeth *et al.* (2001), Chen (2002) and Gesteland (2005).
8 Semiotics is closely related to the field of linguistics. Semiotic theories take signs or sign systems as their object of study when analysing, for example, how human beings construct order in an otherwise chaotic social reality.

Part II
The regional context

3　The Malaysian state and economy in the Southeast Asian region

As discussed in Chapter 1, the various markets and their relative positions within the global economy constitute a landscape from which it is very difficult to decouple. Furthermore, it is a dynamic economic and political landscape that consists of a few 'spikes' such as Japan, South Korea, Taiwan, Hong Kong and Singapore, just to mention the most prominent; several 'hills', including Malaysia, Indonesia, Thailand, the Philippines and Vietnam; and some 'valleys': Cambodia, Laos and Burma. Interestingly, the nation-states in the last category are generally strong but withdrawn in terms of international engagement, whereas the states in the 'hills' are vigorously competing against each other to become the highest 'hill' in the region in terms of economic performance. This makes the markets in this part of the world quite volatile even though they are at the same time organised into various pan-Asian organisations such as ASEAN, ASEAN+3 and AFTA.[1] So we are dealing with nation-states that can be categorised as being in a state of co-opetition when talking about 'hilly' states. In this section I shall zoom in on Malaysia, a country that is a politically stable and economically dynamic 'hill' in Southeast Asia. In particular, I will attempt to identify the drivers behind its development as well as to assess its potential for decoupling from the global economy, in case it finds a need to, politically, economically or otherwise.

The Malaysian economy can be classified as one of the best-performing emerging markets in Southeast Asia. The Economist Intelligence Unit's October 2012 report on Malaysia[2] forecasts Malaysia's political stability during the period 2011–2015 will come under moderate threat, not because of any major shift in the balance of power, but rather owing to internal strife within the two main political alliances. Fiscal policy will be tightened gradually during the forecast period, as the government strives to balance its budget by 2020. Monetary policy will also become tighter as domestic demand strengthens. The economy was expected to resume a fairly stable growth path following a mild recession in 2009 and a rather strong rebound in 2010, a growth trajectory that that is still true for 2014 and beyond. The Economist Intelligence Unit's country report for Malaysia from August 2014 forecast that the economy is to remain on a steady growth path in 2014 to 2018. They expect real GDP expansion to accelerate to 5.7 per cent this year, up from 4.7 per cent in 2013. In relation to inflation, they expect the average rate of consumer price inflation to accelerate to

3.3 per cent in 2014, up from 2.1 per cent in 2013. The government plans to rationalise the country's extensive subsidy schemes and this will push up consumer prices. Despite the faster pace of growth in merchandise imports than in exports, Malaysia will continue to post substantial trade and current-account surpluses in the forecast period.

3.1   Malaysia: a declining 'hill'?

Taking these macroeconomic and policy predictions at face value, Malaysia can be defined as a fairly stable and sound 'hill'. This is especially true for Penang, one of the dynamic 'sub-hills' in the Malaysian economic landscape, because of its heavy focus on manufacturing and automation in various high-tech industry sectors, especially in the electrical and electronic sector (Araffin 2011). However, there is another side to this story. Zooming further in on Penang, the picture becomes more complex. Poh Heem Heem, from the Penang Skills Development Centre (PSDC), agrees that economically speaking, Malaysia is ahead of most of its ASEAN competitors, mainly in the export of commodities and in the electronic components sector. However, according to Poh, the rate of this progress has slowed, which she attributes to Malaysia being caught in the so-called middle income trap (Poh 2010: 46).[3] In response to the predictions put forward in the 2011 Economist Intelligence Unit's report, she characterises the Malaysian economy as exhibiting more problematic developments, including an erosion of its competitive base, a minor increase in private investments, a decline in productivity and a serious 'brain drain' within both academia and industry (Yeah 2011). Poh's advice to the state government is that Penang and Malaysia in general must boost the value-added dimension of its exports if it is not to lose its status as a strong, growth-oriented economy (Poh 2010: 46).

One of the defining features of the middle income trap is a lack of industrial innovation. During fieldwork in Penang in March 2011, I discussed this issue with several informants in the automation industry. The main issues were whether there was a lack of innovative capability on behalf of the workforce or whether there is a lack of an innovative environment in Penang. The informants believe that there are many talented and innovative people in Penang. This was also stressed by researchers from the Penang Institute, one of the main Penang think tanks, who also stressed a need for industrial innovation. They perceived the lack of innovation as partly a result of complacency by entrepreneurs and partly as a consequence of the current full-employment situation, which, according to informants, does not encourage innovative thinking. Along with the high cost of developing new products, this results mainly in industries further elaborating on already existing products instead of creating new ones. According to informants, this is not what industrial innovation is all about, as it does not help the industry or the Penang economy move up the value chain. Only new and cutting-edge products have the capacity to do that. Interestingly, this notion of innovation is supported by *The Global Competitiveness Report 2012–2013* (World Economic Forum 2012).[4]

3.2 From reaction to proaction: the Malaysian federal government's response

Both the Malaysian federal government and the Penang state government are well aware of the difference in outlook between the predictions for growth as formulated in the Economist Intelligence Unit's May 2012 report and the more critical insights that domestic researchers air about the state of the Malaysian economy and the Penang state economy in particular. To counter the critical voices, the federal government has designed what it calls a 'New Economic Model' (NEM). The NEM is a national master plan to operationalise the Economic Transformation Programme (ETP).[5] The NEM consists of a series of strategic reform initiatives proposed by the National Economic Advisory Council to facilitate economic change.

The NEM approach takes a liberal orientation towards the market to further open it up to foreign as well as domestic investors (see Table 3.1). There is an emphasis on economic growth led by the private sector, localised decision making and a preference for technologically capable industries and firms, thus providing the background to attract more FDI. Gone are centralised strategic planning, state participation in the economy and restrictions on foreign skilled workers. The shadow from the developmental state that hovers over the 'old approach' seems to have disappeared. The recommendations for the 'new approach' in the NEM fit very well into the current developmental tendencies in the global economy, where trade liberalisation and open markets are the dominant issues on the agenda.

The main tenet of the NEM is a deeper engagement in the global economy, thus promoting a higher degree of integration and a higher degree of interdependency with the global economy. Because of this 'open door' economic policy, it becomes

Table 3.1 2010 Introducing the New Economic Model (NEM): a new approach to economic development

Old Approach	New Approach
Growth through capital accumulation	Growth through productivity
Dominant state participation in the economy (CME)	Private sector-led growth (LME)
Centralised strategic planning	Local autonomy in decision making
Balanced regional growth	Cluster- and corridor-based economic activities
Specific industries and firms favoured	Technological capable industries and firms favoured
Export dependence on G-3 markets	Asian and Middle-Eastern orientation
Restrictions on foreign skilled workers	Efforts to attract and retain skilled professionals

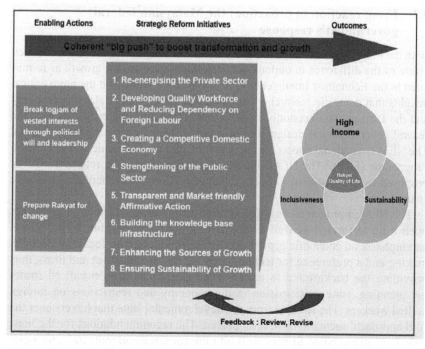

Figure 3.1 The new economic model: enablers and strategic reform initiatives
Source: *Penang Economic Monthly,* June 2010: 49.

harder for the Malaysian state to employ a political and/or economic approach based on decoupling from its global engagement to nurture more domestic developmental schemes and interests. Figure 3.1 shows how the NEM will go about operationalising the strategic reform initiatives.

The basic premise of the strategic reform initiatives is that vested interests in the national economy have created a logjam that is blocking economic transformation and growth and that the Malaysian people must be prepared for the upcoming changes. Eight strategic reform initiatives have been developed to transform the economy in such a way that together they will lead to higher growth. This will result in a constructive triangulation of high income, economic sustainability and social and political inclusiveness, resulting in improved quality of life. The checks and balances in this system are feedback mechanisms, which should lead to a review and an eventual revision of the whole developmental process, thus ensuring a maximum positive impact on the Malaysian economy and ultimately on the Malaysian society. Before assessing the viability of these federal government measures, it is important to position the Malaysian economy in relation to other nation-states in the region to provide us with a measurement against which we can assess Malaysia's economic performance.

3.3 Measuring the economic performance of Malaysia in a Southeast Asian context

As mentioned in Chapter 1, one of the main themes to be developed here is a model of economic triangulation to delineate an increasing interdependency between global and local markets, thus demonstrating the problems behind the argument that it is possible to decouple national economic initiatives from the global economy. Before going further into detail, it is important to provide some background data on Malaysia in relation to other nations within the Southeast Asian region. Employing figures and charts from *The Global Competitiveness Report 2012–2013,*[6] I have adopted a stage model for measuring the level of Malaysia's competitiveness in a Southeast Asian context (Figure 3.2).

Furthermore, I have selected four Southeast Asian countries to compare with Malaysia in a Southeast Asian context (Table 3.2). Singapore has been left out of the equation, as it is economically speaking far above the other Southeast Asian countries in terms of economic development and should instead be related to other countries such as Hong Kong, South Korea and Taiwan. Furthermore, Laos and Burma are not included here because of lack of sufficient data. The four selected countries are Indonesia, Thailand, Vietnam and Cambodia. The reason for including Cambodia is to show the span between the selected countries.

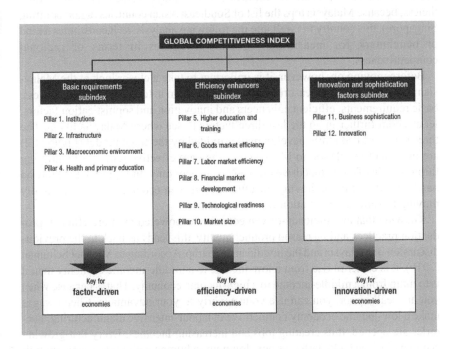

Figure 3.2 The global competitiveness index framework

Table 3.2 Ranking of selected Southeast Asian nations according to *The Global Competitiveness Report 2012–2013*

	Competitiveness Index I2011–2012	Competitiveness Index II 2012–2013	Basic Requirements	Efficient Enhancers	Innovation and Sophistication Factors
Malaysia	21 in 2011–2012*	25 in 2012–2013*	27	23	23
Indonesia	46 in 2011–2012	50 in 2012–2013	58	58	40
Thailand	39 in 2011–2012	38 in 2012–2013	45	47	55
Vietnam	65 in 2011–2012	75 in 2012–2013	91	71	90
Cambodia	97 in 2011–2012	87 in 2012–2013	97	85	72

(* Switzerland was/is ranked 1)

Despite a declining trend in most indicators, probably due to the current global economic crisis, Malaysia still leads in all four categories. However, Thailand and Indonesia are not far behind, and Vietnam is catching up quickly with Malaysia, Indonesia and Thailand and thus could be a serious player in the near future. Nonetheless, because Malaysia tops the list of Southeast Asian countries (again omitting Singapore), this country fits well into the following analysis, as it constitutes a kind of benchmark for measuring the other countries in terms of regional competitiveness.

Before moving on, however, it is important to take a closer look at the Malaysian economy. Having measured Malaysia's position in terms of competitiveness, basic requirements, efficient enhancers and innovation and sophistication factors, let us zoom further in on the last three factors to see where Malaysia fits in. The three stages of economic development provided by the stage model (Figure 3.2) are important in relation to Malaysia, as they are effective tools for identifying the underlying factors that drive the Malaysian economy. In Figure 3.3, Malaysia has been identified as having an efficiency-driven economy that is gradually moving towards an innovation-driven economy.

Knowing that an efficiency-driven economy is powered by more efficient production practices and increased product quality, this leads us back to the previous discussion of Malaysia and the middle income trap. According to Michael Schuman (2010), it is easier to rise from a low-income to a middle-income economy than it is to jump from a middle-income to a high-income economy. That is because when you are really poor, you can use your poverty to your advantage. Cheap wages make a low-income economy competitive in labour-intensive manufacturing. Factories are opened, thus creating jobs and increasing incomes. Every fast-growing economy in Asia kick-started its development in human welfare this way, including Malaysia (Schuman 2010).

Stage of development

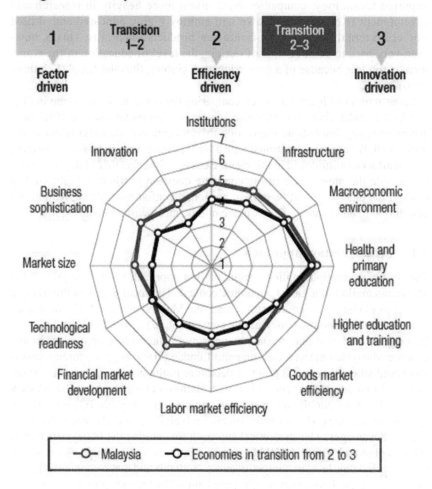

Figure 3.3 Positioning Malaysia in the state model
Source: *The Global Competitiveness Report 2012–2013*, p. 246.

However, that growth model eventually runs out of steam. As income increases, so do costs, undermining the competitiveness of the old, low-tech manufacturing industries. Countries like Malaysia then move up the value chain, into exports of more technologically advanced products, such as electronics. However, according to Schuman, even that is not enough to avoid the 'trap'. To get to the next level, the high-income level, an economy needs to do more than just produce commodities by employing people and investing money in new factories. The economy has to innovate and use labour and capital more productively as well as in new ways. That requires an entirely different way of doing business. Instead of just assembling products designed by others with imported technology, companies must invest more heavily in research and development (R&D) on their own and employ highly educated and skilled workers to turn those investments into new products and profits. This is, however, very hard to achieve if, for example, the level of education of the workforce is too low because of a poor education system, thus the 'trap' (Schuman 2010).

Let us return to Figure 3.3. When comparing the countries in transition indication in the spider chart, that is, those economies that move from an efficiency-driven economy towards an innovation-driven economy Malaysia is not doing badly at all. We are thus confronted with a well-driven economy that is performing well in all sectors employed in this chart. Because of the fact that Malaysia is plotted outside the inner circle in the chart the question is whether Malaysia has reached the outer limits of its current economic configration, taking Schuman's description of an economy caught in the middle income trap into account.

3.4   A triangulation approach

The following section applies a triangulation approach to the analysis of the Malaysian market in a global economic context. The focal points in the triangle consist of (1) how foreign investors 'read' the Malaysian market, (2) the impact of the national economic policy in this context and (3) domestic societal factors. In order to 'read' and thus prepare a company to enter a foreign market, in this case the Malaysian market, Dunning and Lundan (2009) suggest, foreign investors could take a theoretical point of departure in the eclectic paradigm, the so-called OLI paradigm, and combine it with Barney's (1991) resource-based view (RBV). The OLI paradigm consists of three levels. They are (O) ownership-specific advantages, (L) location-specific advantages and (I) internalisation-specific advantages. This theoretical approach for entering the Malaysian market can be combined with the RBV to update, reinforce and maintain a company's resources and thus level of competitiveness. With this and macroeconomic figures as outlined in the Economist Intelligence Unit's 2012 report, plus key economic figures provided by the Malaysian national economic statistical bureau, a 'firm-specific' analysis of the Malaysian market can be carried out. This approach will provide a given company with clear indications of whether to invest in that particular market.

Applying this approach to the Malaysian market, the positive macroeconomic figures might encourage foreign investors to invest despite the fact that some domestic researchers from the PSDC and Penang Institute point to the problematic state of affairs with a slowing of FDI, a small increase in domestic productivity and a decrease in international competitiveness. However, as we have seen, the federal government is already addressing these critical issues through the NEM strategy, and the Penang state government is providing economic facilitators such as the Penang Development Corporation, investPenang and the PSDC to boost productivity and innovation.

Turning to the second point in the triangle, societal factors, foreign investors might combine the OLI and RBV with an institutional theoretical approach as developed by North (1991), Peng (2002) and in particular Scott (2008, 2010). Here the emphasis is not on key economic data but rather on the Malaysian institutional environment. This includes how the two main categories of societal institutions relate to and impact each other. Formal institutions consist of more or less well-defined and enforced rules and regulations in relation to the juridical system, industrial and political development schemes, educational and social welfare systems and so forth. Informal institutions include religion, culturally defined value systems, collectivist and family-oriented social systems and so forth.

Defining the Malaysian market as an emerging market, Peng (2002) states that, in general, informal institutions have a great impact on the functionality, implementation and applicability of formal institutions, thus making the overall society more or less unstable. If an investor employs institutional theory to the Malaysian market, the perspective would not be as bright as when looking at it through the key economic data. The problems uncovered through this theoretical lens consist of a severe brain and capital drain,[7] problematic relations between the Malay, Chinese and Indian ethnic groups, increasing sociopolitical internalisation of a radicalising Islam, tight control of public opinion through the employment of the Security Offences (Special Measures) Act, introduced in August 2012, that replaced the Internal Security Act (ISA),[8] and tensions between the federal and (especially opposition-run) state governments,[9] just to mention some of the findings that such an analysis would reveal. By combining the key findings from the OLI/RBV and institutional analyses, foreign investors can thus obtain deep insights into how the Malaysian market and society respectively function as well as how the two societal sectors relate to each other. As a consequence of these analyses, foreign investors might adopt a 'wait and see' approach to investment in the Malaysian market because of the insecurities delineated in the societal sectors, even though the key economic data show a positive tendency. After all, seen from the foreign investors' perspective, if they are to invest in the Malaysian market, they want to be reasonably sure of a positive return on their investment over time.

Arguably, a triangulation of the global and the national economies combined with an analysis of the societal context in which both the global and national economies are embedded constitutes a powerful tool to analyse the constitution of, in this case, a 'hilly' and dynamic socio-economic landscape. Because of the findings from the institutional analysis of the Malaysian society, an observer is prompted to ask, who the main beneficiaries of the NEM economic policy are: international investors or the national/local entrepreneurs. If one takes another look at Table 3.1, where the NEM approach to national economic development is outlined, the 'new' economic approach is based on an almost neo-liberal policy. The 'nursing', that is, developmental state is out, and in comes (global) open market forces that, besides introducing a minimal neo-liberal type of state, also have a fragmenting effect on the Malaysian/Penang market, thus increasing the competitive level there. For example, the Penang state government is very focused on attracting FDI to finance its development schemes. This leaves out, for example, those SMEs that are not capable of attracting FDI or contributing to it by not being either subcontractors or suppliers to MNCs.[10]

The development of socio-economic fault-lines within the local SME community is therefore a likely outcome of such a developmental scheme, thus creating the elements for a non-coherent domestic market that constitutes an easy target for predatory international business interests. From this perspective, the NEM and its various economic initiatives do not lift the Malaysian economy out of the middle income trap in which it currently finds itself, nor does it help domestic businesses move up the value chain. The NEM seems to be designed as a tool to attract more FDI, as this constitutes the principal source for (re-)fuelling further domestic economic development. If Malaysia is to avoid losing its current status as a fast-developing 'hill' in an otherwise dynamic 'hilly' Southeast Asian economic landscape, then it has to start addressing the social and political problems in the informal sector highlighted in the institutional analysis. Potential global investors might not like what they find there. In order to go further into the Malaysian case, in the next section I will focus on how Penang state fits into the Malaysian national context.

3.5   Penang's economic and political environment in a Malaysian context

When discussing the economic and political environment in Penang, it is important to position Penang state in the national political and economic environment, especially in relation to the so-called Northern Corridor Economic Region (NCER) that consists of the four states Pelis, Kedah, Penang and the northern part of the state Perak. Malaysia is currently divided into four so-called developmental corridors identified under the Ninth Malaysia Plan: the Eastern Corridor Economic Region (ECER), consisting of the states of Terengganu, Kelantan and Pahang; the Iskandar Development Region (IDR), also known as the South Johor Economic Region, and the Sabah-Sarawak Corridor. In July 2007, Prime Minister Abdullah Ahmad Badawi (2003–2009) launched the fourth developmental corridor, the Northern Corridor Economic Region (NCER).[11] During the launch, Badawi emphasised that:

> The north of Malaysia is a region rich in resources and potential. If the region is given opportunity to flourish, the country's overall competitiveness will be strengthened and prosperity will be better distributed. This is the main rationale for the formation of the Northern Corridor Economic Region. The development of the Northern Corridor will also focus attention on social issues such as rural development, agriculture modernisation and poverty. These are areas that must be addressed with improved, market-led approaches. To this end, the Northern Corridor Blueprint was spearheaded by private sector input to ensure the development of commercially sustainable measures and programmes.[12]

The Northern Corridor Blueprint contained three main economic thrusts: agriculture, manufacturing and services. Its goal was to transform the northern region into a dynamic region over a period of eighteen years, from 2007 to 2025. The implementation of the plan was divided into three phases. The first aimed to lay the foundation by securing anchor investors and constructing priority infrastructure. The second phase aimed to strengthen efforts in broadening and deepening private sector involvement as well as business networks and linkages. The third and final phase of the development blueprint was to establish technology and achieve regional market leadership through sustainable market-led growth. A total of RM 177 billion was deemed needed to implement key NCER initiatives over the eighteen-year period, with two-thirds of the investment expected to come from the private sector, including private finance initiatives.

From the blueprint we can summarise the main expectations for NCER. The regional approach is to secure a balanced economic development between the four states, thus closing the development and income gap within the region. The strategy behind the implementation of NCER is to be market-driven and private sector led. The main reason for this is to create new resources for growth especially within agriculture, manufacturing and service sectors. Most important, the NCER initiative seeks to accelerate the selected sectors towards higher value-added activities such as design and R&D. Finally, in terms of logistics, the NCER is strategically located within the Indonesia–Malaysia–Thailand growth triangle.

The NCER was partly intended to capitalise on the existing strength of the region, rather than creating new economic activities. This approach was believed to have a greater chance of achieving the desired outcome and less lead time was thus required. For instance, Penang is the choice of numerous leading global manufacturers with more than three decades of industrialisation experience. It made sense to promote Penang as the regional logistics hub because the entire logistic solution of facilitation and services for land, sea and air were already in place. Penang's main contribution to the NCER was and still is in high-end (health) tourism, electronic manufacturing and R&D.[13]

3.5.1 Societal organisation in Penang

Penang state is geographically and administratively divided into two sections: Penang Island, which is 293 square kilometres and located in the Straits of Malacca, and Seberang Perai (also known as Province Wellesley), which is a narrow strip of 738 square kilometres on the Malay peninsula across a narrow channel, four kilometres at its narrowest point. It is bordered by the state Kedah in the north and east and the state of Perak in the south.

The strait between Penang Island and Seberang Perai is called the North Channel. It is positioned to the north of Georgetown, the Penang state capital. The strait to the south of Georgetown is the South Channel. Penang Island itself is irregularly shaped, with a granite-filled soil, and is quite hilly and forested. The highest point is Western Hill (part of Penang Hill), which reaches 830 metres

Table 3.3 Breakdown of ethnic groups in the state of Penang

Ethnic Group ('000)	2006	2007	2008	2009	2010	2011
Malaysian:	1,407.4	1,426.6	1,448.2	1,471.9	1,497.7	1,484.8
Malays	612.3	625.3	639.3	654.3	670.1	643.8
Other Bumiputera	5.6	6.0	6.2	6.5	6.8	4.9
Chinese	635.3	639.8	645.3	651.6	658.7	668.7
Indians	148.0	149.3	151.0	153.1	155.6	160.7
Others	6.2	6.2	6.4	6.4	6.5	6.7
Non-Malaysian Citizens	85.0	91.8	98.6	105.4	112.2	126.8
Total	1,492.4	1,518.5	1,546.8	1,577.3	1,609.9	1,611.6

above sea level. The coastal plains are narrow, the most extensive of which is in the northeast, which forms a triangular promontory where Georgetown is situated. Province Wellesley is mostly flat. Butterworth, the main city in Province Wellesley, lies along the mouth of the Perai River and faces Georgetown at a distance of three kilometres across the channel to the east. The state has the highest population density in Malaysia with about 2,032 people per square kilometre on the island and about 866 people per square kilometre on the mainland. Penang is the only state in Malaysia where ethnic Chinese form a majority. Malaysia is a multicultural country divided into three main ethnic groups, plus mixed groups termed rather anonymously 'others', that is, representatives from other ethnic groups originating outside Malaysia. In 2010, the ethnic composition of Malaysia consisted of 65 per cent ethnic Malays, 26 per cent ethnic Chinese, 7 per cent ethnic Indians and 2 per cent 'others'. Table 3.3 shows the breakdown of ethnic groups in the State of Penang.

Being one of the earliest, most established urban centres in Malaysia, Penang prides itself on its progress, while at the same time relishing its traditional and enduring values, way of life and mannerisms. Chinese influence has always been more evident in urban areas because of their greater numbers; the Malays, until recent times, have largely resided in the rural areas in the south and south-western part of the island. Malays consider themselves a minority group in Penang, although they have special rights since the early 1970s through the affirmative action programme.[14]

Twenty-first-century Penang is a thriving commercial and industrial centre with a relatively high standard of living. However, in terms of development, it has been overtaken in recent years by the Klang Valley close to Kuala Lumpur, which is currently the political and economic heart of modern Malaysia. While the slower rate of development in Penang has left much of its cultural and architectural heritage intact, the development that has taken place has been poorly managed because of a lack of adequate funding, especially infrastructure funding provided exclusively by the federal government and a low level of participatory local government since the late 1960s. Nonetheless, Penangites maintain a strong civic identity rooted in Penang's former pre-eminence, reinforced by a strong local cultural and linguistic identity. This identity was reinforced on 7 July 2008, when Georgetown, together with Malacca, was formally inscribed as a UNESCO World Heritage Site. It is officially recognised as having a unique architectural and cultural townscape without parallel anywhere in East and Southeast Asia, a status that civil groups and NGOs capitalise on in their work to preserve the uniqueness of Georgetown against predatory developers.

3.5.2 The political environment in Penang

Penang state has its own state legislature and executive, but these have limited powers compared to those of the Malaysian federal authorities. As a former British settlement, Penang is one of only four states in Malaysia not to have a hereditary Malay ruler or sultan, the other three being Malacca, also a former British settlement whose sultanate was ended by the Portuguese conquest in 1511, and the Borneo states of Sabah and Sarawak.

The head of the state executive is a *Yang di-Pertua Negeri* (governor) appointed by the *Yang di-Pertuan Agong* (King of Malaysia). The present governor is Tun Dato' Seri Haji Abdul Rahman bin Haji Abbas. In practice, the governor is a figurehead and he acts on the advice of the State Executive Council, which is appointed from the majority party in the Legislative Assembly. The chief minister, currently Lim Guan Eng, who is the fourth chief minister of the State of Penang,[15] heads the State Executive Council, the highest administrative body in the state, which again answers to the Legislative Assembly. The State Secretariat and other state or federal government departments assist the Executive Council in the state administration. Most of the main government offices are housed in the sixty-five-storey Tun Abdul Razak Complex (KOMTAR) with several branches of the administration spread throughout Georgetown.

There have been occasional calls by the United Malays National Organisation (UMNO), members of the ruling coalition, *Barisan Nasional* (BN), to rotate the position of chief minister between BN component parties, but this has consistently been rejected by the BN leadership. This demand reached new heights in 2006 on allegations of marginalisation by the Malay populace. Interestingly, one of the more vocal proponents was Khairy Jamaludin, the son-in-law of the previous Malaysian prime minister Badawi. During Mahathir Mohamad's tenure as prime minister (1981–2003), Mahathir refuted claims of marginalisation by alluding to the Malay-governed state of Kelantan. In fact, Malays in Penang are second only to their counterparts in the Klang Valley.

3.5.3 The economic organisation of Penang

When discussing the economic development of Penang, one has to distinguish between pre- and post-1971. Before 1971, Penang was mainly an agricultural economy complemented by import substitution businesses. This was to ensure that the local economy could stay independent and produce enough for local consumption. As there were no manufacturing companies and the British companies, mainly in trading and plantations, did not restore their operations to the pre-war level after WWII, unemployment was high during that period, at about 16.4 per cent. Furthermore, Penang lost its free port status in 1969. To revamp the economy, in 1969 the Penang state government, headed by Tun Lim Chong Eu, identified the electronics industry as having the best potential to absorb the state's excess semi-skilled labour force. Developing the agriculture sector further was out of the question as land has always been a scarce commodity because of the geography of the island.

After 1971 things changed radically. To create extra incentives to attract labour-intensive industries from abroad, the Free Trade Zones Act was passed in April 1971 after close consultation between state and federal agencies. Two zones were created in Penang, one in Seberang Perai for heavy industries and another for cleaner industries in Bayan Baru.[16] The south-eastern part of the island became highly industrialised. From the original eight pioneer electrical and electronics firms, also called the Eight Samurais – Intel, AMD, Osram, Hitachi, Clarion, Agilent Technologies, Robert Bosch and Fairchild Semiconductors – more than 200 other MNC high-tech electronic plants such as Dell, Altera, Motorola, Plexus and Seagate moved in. They are all located within the Bayan Lepas Free Industrial Zone, which was established in 1972 in Bayan Baru. Based on the MNCs, Penang has thus concentrated mainly on information and communication technology (ICT), semiconductors, computer and computer peripherals, data storage devices, telecommunications equipment (software) and consumer electronics. To service the MNCs there were in 2010 2,614 SMEs in the manufacturing sector in Penang working as suppliers, subcontractors or independent companies located within and outside Bayan Lepas.[17] They have specialised mainly in automation, plastics, precision engineering and metalwork, chemical products and packaging of various kinds.

As a consequence of these developments, today Penang state has the fourth largest economy among the states in Malaysia, after Perak, Selangor and Johor. Manufacturing is the most important component of the Penang economy, contributing about 49 per cent of the state's GDP in 2011 and 8.5 per cent of the national GDP that same year.[18] This is quite impressive as Penang only constitutes about 6 per cent of the total Malaysian population.[19] In January 2005, Penang was formally accorded the Multimedia Super Corridor Cyber City status (MSC), the first outside of Cyberjaya on mainland Malaysia, with the aim of setting up high-tech industrial parks to conduct cutting-edge ICT research. Leveraging the infrastructure that has made it Malaysia's foremost electronic hub, Penang is poised to take off in the highly promising frontier of biotechnology. This new initiative is in line with the Ninth Malaysia Plan, which has identified this sector as one of the main areas to help drive the country forward to a developed knowledge-based economy as required by the Cyber City status.

In recent years, however, the state has experienced a gradual decline in FDI due to factors such as cheaper labour costs in Vietnam, China and India, and arguably, lagging human capital in the form of a well-educated and up-to-date labour force. Furthermore, the *entrepôt* trade has declined, in part because of the loss of Penang's free port status in 1969, but also because of the active development of Port Klang, near Kuala Lumpur. However, the container terminal in Butterworth is to undergo a major upgrade, as detailed in the NCER plan; it will mainly service the northern region but still cater to the rest of Malaysia, in competition with Port Klang.[20] Other important sectors of Penang's economy that will be upgraded include health tourism, which is mainly clustered in the northern and eastern parts of Penang Island and in Georgetown, together with finance, shipping and other service sectors.

3.6 Penang state government's economic policies (2000 and onwards)

To counter the industrial decline, the Penang state government initiated an aggressive economic policy. Even though Penang received MSC status in 2005, high-tech industry in Penang still faces stiff competition from the original MSC on the Malaysia mainland, thus threatening its position as Malaysia's 'Silicon Island'. The Chinese-led political party in Penang, the Gerakan Party, which led the state government from 1969 to 2008, took several steps to address this threat. According to Peggy Teo, selling Penang is therefore an important element in the government's industrial strategy and was furthermore in line with the economic visions promoted by both Vision 2020[21] and MSC for developing a new Malaysia. Penang has thus stepped up its own plans to become a symbol of this emerging era (Teo 2003: 554).

In 1992, the Penang Development Corporation (PDC)[22] was asked to develop a road map to operationalise the main ideas behind Vision 2020. In drawing on this vision, the PDC developed the theme 'Penang: Into the 21st Century' to outline its goals. It first aimed to diversify Penang's economy by creating a competitive high-tech local manufacturing capability, thereby responding to the demands from the various MNCs. The second goal was to develop a sophisticated services sector buttressed by 'state-of-the-art' technology and skills. The third goal was to modernise and upgrade productive capabilities in the agricultural sector. To achieve these three goals, five strategic thrusts were identified:

1. Develop a dynamic, resilient and progressive economy in which the industrial base is more capital, skill and technology intensive, that promotes small and medium enterprises and will enhance tourism and modernise the agricultural sector.
2. Protect and conserve the environment.
3. Foster a more equitable society and cultivate integration.
4. Enhance Penang's role as a regional centre.
5. Upgrade the administration mechanism to support industry.

(Teo 2003:554)

The Penang state government, strongly supported by the private sector, initiated several projects that laid the groundwork to achieve these five strategies. For example, two Free Industrial Zones and five industrial parks were developed, covering 1850 ha of land on both Penang Island and Port Wellesley on the mainland. Tax incentive schemes were introduced to entice foreign capital. A highly diversified electronics industry as well as many supporting industries in engineering, metal, plastics and packaging for the industry were courted together with industries in the textile and apparel sectors.

As a result MNCs have been attracted to Penang because of its good human resources, an efficient transport and communication infrastructure and a well-functioning banking and insurance sector, as well as good freight and forwarding services. Automation was encouraged right from the start to keep labour costs down. The Penang state government has been supportive of foreign investment and has proven an important facilitator in the business sector. So successful has the Penang state programme been in engineering itself as a progressive and investor-friendly state, that manufacturing increased from 13 per cent of GDP in 1970 to 49 per cent of the Penang GDP in 2011,[23] employing more than 40 per cent of the total labour force.[24]

3.7   Industrial facilitators

Besides providing tax and non-tax incentive packages for both local industries and MNCs, the Penang state government has introduced two industrial facilitators to strengthen the work of the PDC: investPenang and the Penang Institute. These two institutions are described later, as they will be integrated into a more general discussion on how various types of economic facilitators and government initiatives impact the Chinese SME business community.

3.7.1   investPenang

Established by the Penang state government on 5 November 2004, investPenang is a non-profit organisation with the sole purpose of promoting local and international investments in Penang.[25] The organisation aims to promote sustainable business relations, rejuvenate and encourage further business activity through continued investments in pertinent sectors, and explore new areas with growth potential that are profitable in both the short and long term.

To ensure sustainable development, investPenang performs the following functions: a) provides information and resources to investors, b) enhances Penang's business-friendly environment, c) strengthens Penang's competitive edge, d) promotes investment, e) supports existing companies' growth and f) facilitates the growth of domestic industries.

As head of one of the most urbanised states in Malaysia, the Penang state government's main focus is to make Penang the location of choice for business enterprises, a destination of choice for tourists and visitors and a habitat of choice for those who desire sustainable living. investPenang works in close collaboration with federal government agencies such as the Malaysian Industrial Development Authority (MIDA), Malaysia External Trade Development Corporation (MATRADE), Small and Medium Industries Development Corporation (SMIDEC), Multimedia Development Corporation (MDC), Malaysian Biotechnology Corporation and others to help investors get permits and licences as well as providing business incentives. At the state level, investPenang collaborates with the state government and local governments to ensure ease of doing business for investors throughout the state.

The KPMG's 'Exploring Global Frontiers' report (2009)[26] identified Penang as one of the thirty-one business process outsourcing locations of the future because of the availability of skilled labour, niche specialisations and government incentives. Likewise, the United Nations Industrial Development Organisation (UNIDO) in its Industrial Development Report 2009, rated Penang as one of the ten most dynamic industrial cluster locations in the world, having demonstrated a successful manufacturing experience among developing economies. These industrial cluster locations have created a conducive investment environment, generated employment and are able to compete in the international market. The recognition given by KPMG and UNIDO, together with the availability of investment and trade incentives such as pioneer status, tax holidays and bilateral agreements with Malaysia's trading partners, provide abundant benefits to existing and potential investors. Political stability and the proactive stance taken by both the federal and state governments are expected to ensure that investment ventures are safe, protected and respected.

3.7.2 Penang institute

Penang Institute was formerly known as the Socio-Economic and Environmental Research Institute (SERI). It was established in 1997 as an independent, non-profit, Penang-based research institute with a focus on facilitating sustainable, continuous and balanced development for the State of Penang. From the beginning SERI was a unique institution. Unlike many other larger think tanks, SERI retained its compact structure and slim organisation, allowing the institute to respond rapidly to new challenges. Over time, SERI firmly established itself as one of Malaysia's leading independent think tanks, regularly consulted by the government and local and international NGOs on a diverse range of issues from education and sustainability to economic and human resource issues.[27]

In August 2011, responding to new political and economic challenges, SERI underwent a transformation that included a name change. It is now known as the Penang Institute. Building on SERI's reputation as a centre of excellence, Penang Institute aspires to be one of the best policy research institutes in the region, one that will provide both the Penang state government and the people of Penang with far-sighted and innovative policy options for Penang. Research and publishing continues to be Penang Institute's core business. Its focus in the coming years is to imagine what Penang would look like as a successful international city in the heart of Asia. The institute thus aims to provide viable alternatives to existing problems and anticipates future challenges by thinking ahead to make Penang the cultural, economic and intellectual capital of the region.

The institute pursues three main activities. The first is policy research. The main focus in the next few years is to position the institute in the forefront of the policy-making process by providing research-driven policy inputs, leveraging its traditional strength in data collection and analysis and complementing it with acute policy analysis. Penang Institute also does studies for state, federal and international agencies, notably the PDC, PSDC, the Ministry of Higher Education and United Nations agencies such as the UNDP. The institute also organises a lecture series to bring together renowned scholars, intellectuals and thinkers from diverse fields to Penang to speak about issues relevant to the state in its historic role as the cultural, intellectual and economic centre of Asia. Finally, as Penang becomes a regional logistical and knowledge hub for the international community, the institute plans to organise a 'Country Update' public seminar series featuring opinion makers and experts who share their insights on various Southeast Asian countries.

3.8   From framework to substance

Having now positioned Malaysia and Penang economically and industrially in the Southeast Asian region and provided some data on how especially Penang is organised both politically and economically the next step is to provide an analytical socio-economic and political framework for how to understand Penang in this context. Before embarking on this, however, it is important to take a closer look at the ethnic Chinese, not only in Malaysia but also in the region per se. Even though the ethnic Chinese constitute a minority in each of the Southeast Asian countries, they have a huge impact on the financial and economic performance in those countries. The following chapter thus discusses different notions of Chineseness, the Chinese diaspora and Chinese network practices in a Southeast Asian multicultural context. This is essential to understand the political and social forces that drive the societal space in which the ethnic Chinese operate in a Malaysian cum Penang context.

Notes

1 For a discussion of East and Southeast Asian pan-regional organisations, see Chapter 1.
2 See http://country.eiu.com/Malaysia. Accessed 15 October 2012.
3 Briefly, the middle income trap is when a country's growth plateaus and eventually stagnates after reaching middle income levels. The problem usually arises when developing economies find themselves stuck in the middle, with rising wages and declining cost competitiveness, unable to compete with advanced economies in high-skill innovations, or with low-income, low-wage economies in the cheap production of manufactured goods. For a discussion of the middle income trap see www.chinalawblog. com/2010/08/china_malaysia_korea_and_the_middle_income_trap.html. Accessed 2 February 2012. I return to this discussion later on in this chapter.
4 See www3.weforum.org/docs/WEF_GlobalCompetitivenessReport_2012–13.pdf. Accessed 2 April 2012.
5 The ETP is one of the 'four pillars'. The other three pillars are: 1Malaysia, the Governmental Transformation Programme (GTP) and the 10th Malaysian Plan 2011–2015. For more details about the ETP see http://etp.pemandu.gov.my/. Accessed 1 February 2013.
6 See www3.weforum.org/docs/WEF_GlobalCompetitivenessReport_2012–13.pdf. Accessed 2 April 2012.
7 Toh Kin Woon in *Penang Economic Monthly,* August 2010, pp. 16–19. See also World Bank (2011), *Malaysia Economic Monitor: Brain Drain.*

8 ISA has been replaced and repealed by the Security Offences (Special Measures) Act 2012 which was passed by the Malaysian parliament and given the royal assent on 18 June 2012. The Act came into force on 31 July 2012.

9 Francis Hutchinson in *Penang Economic Monthly,* July 2010, pp. 8–14.

10 According to Chin (forthcoming), SMEs constitute about 99 per cent of industries in Penang.

11 The following is a summary of the original plan, which is termed 'Northern Corridor Regional Economic Development Blueprint. Growth with Social Equity', May 2007.

12 The following is a summary of the original plan, which is termed 'Northern Corridor Regional Economic Development Blueprint. Growth with Social Equity'. May 2007. Assessed 6 February 2010.

13 For a detailed discussion of NCER, see 'Northern Corridor Economic Region Socio-economic Blueprint'. July 30, 2007 (www.koridorutara.com.my/download/download/Koridor%20Utara%20Blueprint%20(English).pdf). Accessed October 2013.

14 For more details on the affirmative action programme, see Chapters 4 and 5.

15 For a detailed presentation of Lim Guan Eng's political career, see http://en.wikipedia.org/wiki/Lim_Guan_Eng. Accessed 17 March 2012.

16 *Penang Economic Monthly,* October–December 2009.

17 *Banci Ekonomi. Economic Census. Profil Perusahaan Kecil Dan Sedehana. Profile of Small and Medium Enterprise.* Department of Statistics, Malaysia. 2011.

18 *Penang Economic Outlook,* 16 January 2013.

19 *Penang Economic Monthly,* January 2010.

20 For a detailed discussion of the Penang Port and the container terminal in Butterworth see *Penang Monthly,* September 2012, pp. 28–31.

21 *Wawasan 2020* or *Vision 2020* was introduced by Prime Minister Mahathir Mohamad during the tabling of the Sixth Malaysia Plan in 1991. The vision calls for Malaysia to become a self-sufficient industrialised nation by the year 2020, and encompasses all aspects of life, from economic prosperity, social well-being, a world-class educational system and political stability, as well as psychological balance. For more details on Vision 2020 see the official Web page: www.wawasan2020.com/vision/index.html. Accessed 2 February 2012.

22 For more details on the PDC, see http://pdc.gov.my/. 15 January 2011.

23 *Penang Economic Outlook,* 16 January 2013.

24 Although tourism is the second pillar of growth in Penang, this sector will not be discussed in this context as the main focus is on Chinese entrepreneurs. For further readings on the tourism sector, see Peggy Teo 2003.

25 For more details on investPenang, see www.investpenang.gov.my/portal. Accessed 17 March 2012.

26 KPMG. Accessed 17 March 2012.

27 For more details on Penang Institute, see http://penanginstitute.org/v3/home. Accessed 17 March 2012.

4 Towards an understanding of ethnic Chinese in Southeast Asia

Contrary to a general notion that the Chinese of Southeast Asian descent form part of a coherent worldwide ethnic group based on common perceptions of Chinese-ness (Fukuyama 1995; Redding 1996; Ong and Nonini 1997), this chapter argues that the Chinese in Southeast Asia consist of several different socially integrated groups. This differentiation reflects impacts from colonialism, early nation building and contemporary processes of social and political transformations within individual Southeast Asian nations. One negative consequence of this is that ethnic Chinese are subject to various types of 'othering', resulting in, for example, affirmative action policies in Malaysia and social stigmatisation in Indonesia, marking them as a distinct ethnic minority.

Such processes of 'othering' are also reflected in notions of 'Chinese capitalism'. The latter is, according to a culturalist reading, defined as constituting a flow of ethnicised capital governed by age-old Chinese kinship and language associations wrapped up in Confucian dogmas (Yao 2002a). The main *modus operandi* controlling this flow is ascribed to *guanxi* affiliations based on *xinyong* or trust.[1]

This chapter takes a critical stand towards such notions. I argue that Chinese business practices do not typify a specific Chinese economy paralleling the market economy and thus employ an approach that can be characterised as de-essentialising conceptions of 'Chinese capitalism'. By employing such an approach, the notion of Chinese capitalism stands out as an Occidentalised ethnicisation of capitalist practices (see also Gomez 2004; Wee 2004). The main purpose of this chapter is thus to identify and deconstruct such preconceptions.

Furthermore, confining a study of ethnic Chinese and ethnic Chinese entrepreneurship to intra- and/or inter-ethnic relations within a given Southeast Asian community only gives a one-dimensional perspective of ethnic Chinese. This chapter recognises the importance of the international realm that ethnic Chinese also belong to. It thus contrasts the international and domestic aspects of being ethnic Chinese so that their exact societal positioning in a given Southeast Asian country of residence can be assessed.

To gauge how ethnic Chinese switch back and forth between the national and international realms, this chapter discusses processes of diasporisation and de-diasporisation. Of special interest here is Riggs' (2001) notion of 'de-diasporisation', which can be taken to mean being localised without disappearing into the local,[2] a notion that this chapter alternatively defines as 'grounded cosmopolitanism'. For now, it suffices to say that the latter is not constrained by a time dimension as is the case with the notion of diaspora. This means that ethnic Chinese are not sojourners or cyclical migrants to the region but residents and citizens, thus underlining a generational perspective. As discussed later in this chapter, the concept of diaspora seems almost archaic and therefore outdated, both empirically and intellectually, when it is confronted with empirical data from a contemporary Southeast Asian context. I am therefore not concerned with the actual construction of local, national or transnational ethnoscapes as discussed by Appadurai (1991) or supposedly ethnically related diasporic networks like Weidenbaum and Hughes (1996). Rather, I argue that specific sociopolitical developments in a given Southeast Asian community have to be taken into account when trying to understand those processes that activate or de-activate relations to a possible ethnically related transnational community.

This chapter forwards the proposition that in modern global capitalism, there are no simplistic distinctions between the economic, political or cultural spheres. Arguably, the production of identity is related to the production of economic and political power. In this context, ethnic identities become a form of negotiated social capital that is disseminated through existing, in this particular case, more or less truncated, ethnic Chinese (business) networks that contribute to the creation of equally truncated regional and/or transnational non-ethnically affiliated business networks.

On the basis of this, I suggest that, contrary to the general notion of diaspora in a Southeast Asian context, we replace the notion of conventional diaspora with a latent, fragmented and multi-layered outlet that allows ethnic Chinese (entrepreneurs) to relate to their international connections through processes of diasporisation and de-diasporisation, thus endowing the definition of their identity with a cosmopolitan yet locally bounded touch. Furthermore, an impetus for linking or de-linking to the international realm besides business interests is provided by specific social and political developments that either dispel or integrate the individual ethnic Chinese (entrepreneur) in his or her community of residence. Given this societal fluidity, the chapter questions whether *guanxi* affiliations are essential for doing business in either national or international ethnic Chinese business communities, as is argued by Yang (1994), Weidenbaum and Hughes (1996), Yeung (1998) and Luo (2000). This critique becomes even more pertinent, as many writers let *guanxi* affiliations play an all-encompassing and dominating role in discourses on the Chinese diaspora, as it is conceived of as constituting an international transmission belt for ethnic Chinese capital, entrepreneurs, migrants and sojourners (Kotkin 1992; Bolt 2000; McKeown 2001; Callahan 2002).

When taking a critical look at the literature on Chinese business practices and *guanxi*-affiliated networks in East and Southeast Asia, however, it becomes clear that such networks are multidimensional in terms of both meaning and function. For example, Yao (2002b) writes that in China, the term *guanxi* refers to any form of 'relatedness'. It does not have any connotations specifically related to either commercial or political activities. In fact, *guanxi* is a generic term on which phrases representing more specific forms of 'relatedness' are built. Thus, according to Yao, we have *guoji guanxi* or international relations, *routi guanxi* or carnal relations, *fuji guanxi* or marital relations, and so on. These different kinds of *guanxi* vary in terms of their respective emotional depth, social context and ethical bond. The 'social connectedness' in the commercial world thus represents but one type of *guanxi* among many, so therefore we should strictly refer to *shangye guanxi*, or 'commercial *guanxi*', when talking about *guanxi* practices in a business context (Yao 2002b). Thus, when in the following I refer to *guanxi*, it is this kind of *guanxi* I am referring to.

Zooming further in on the relationship between *guanxi* and business, Wong (1998), Gomez and Hsiao (2001), Gomez (2004) and Jacobsen (2004a) have problems finding evidence that dyadic-linked *guanxi*-affiliated business deals in a local, national or transnational context dominate the business field. On the contrary, we find that ethnic Chinese transnational business relations are generally based on ad hoc arrangements and at best on truncated forms of networking practices (Gomez 2004). This means that when Southeast Asian ethnic Chinese entrepreneurs, especially those representing SMEs, decide to transnationalise their business, they might initially connect to fellow Chinese entrepreneurs, either through family connections or previously utilised business connections. After this initial contact they branch out to the local business community in order to 'sink in' and tap local business opportunities. This is what is meant by truncated business networks. These are therefore shallow in terms of time depth and not necessarily confined to intra-ethnic relations, but apply as well to inter-ethnic business relations. Cribb (2000) furthermore contests the hypothesis that the various institutions, norms and practices of ethnic Chinese are the growth engine behind their enterprises (see also Li and Wright 1999). On the contrary, profit motives, combined with a pragmatic reading of a given societal landscape in which to operate, seem to prevail when doing business, be it with intra-ethnic or inter-ethnic partners.

Arguably, *guanxi*-affiliated business practices are thus only one strategy among others employed when initiating (new) business transactions with Chinese or non-Chinese partners in their respective Southeast Asian communities of residence. This hypothesis reflects Arif Dirlik's proposition that an overemphasis on *guanxi*-affiliated business practices is a rhetorically determined ethnicisation of capitalist practices (Dirlik 1996).

4.1   Southeast Asian ethnic Chinese and diasporic practices

In discussing the concept of diaspora, Riggs (2001) points out that we may think of a diaspora as any community of individuals living outside their homeland who identify themselves one way or another with the state or people(s) of that homeland. He continues to stress, however, that rarely, if ever, do diasporans organise as a single collectivity. Consequently, diaspora organisations often clash with each other or simply pursue different goals. It is thus incorrect to reify the notion of a diaspora or speak of it as 'acting' or 'doing' anything. All actions by diasporans are carried out individually or through organised groups of which they are members (Riggs 2001: 1).

This conceptual ambiguity, that is, 'who is doing what, the migrant or the diaspora?', runs like a red thread through the literature on diaspora. Judith Shuval (2000), citing Sheffer (1986), Safran (1991) and Clifford (1994), writes that these authors have all proposed more or less encompassing definitions of the concept of diaspora. Although they are not identical, the critical components of their definitions are a history of dispersal, myths or memories of a homeland, alienation in the host country, desire for an eventual return, ongoing support for the homeland and a collective identity defined by the aforementioned relationship (Shuval 2000: 43).

Concurring with these defining features, she stresses the importance of highlighting the affective-expressive components. According to Shuval, diasporic discourses reflect a sense of being part of an ongoing transnational network that includes dispersed people who retain a sense of their uniqueness and an interest in their homeland. She continues:

> A diaspora is . . . a social construct founded on feeling, consciousness, memory, mythology, history, meaningful narratives, group identity, longings, dreams, allegorical and virtual elements, all of which play an important role in establishing a diaspora reality. At a given moment in time, the sense of connection to a homeland must be strong enough to resist forgetting, assimilating or distancing.
>
> (Shuval 2000: 43)

The main problem with these definitions is that they are very encompassing and feeble when compared to the real-life situations that migrants face, thereby running the risk of losing out as being ideational explanatory frameworks and/or solutions towards a given concrete and thus localised problem. For example, Shuval's emphasis on the affective-expressive components of migrants' relations to a given homeland seems to present linking up to a diaspora as a possible solution to a problem. However, when talking about Southeast Asians of Chinese descent, emotional expressions in relation to a given grievance do not necessarily imply any references to a given homeland. Rather they are emotional expressions in relation to localised and concrete sociopolitical economic events that in one way or another affect the 'life situation' of the individual migrant turned permanent resident or citizen. Such grievances with respect to specific events in their community of residence do not make those people diasporic in relation to most of the aforementioned defining features of diaspora. The question we therefore have to ask is whether a potential longing for a distant or mythical 'homeland' is important and how widespread this actually is among migrants turned permanent residents or citizens. Perhaps it is more widespread in theoretical extrapolations of diasporic practices than in real life! For example, in a response to Leo Suryadinata, Tan Chee Beng states:

> As proud citizens of our respective countries, we feel insulted to be called or even referred to as 'Overseas Chinese'. We are overseas in China but not when we are at home in Malaysia, Indonesia, the Philippines, and so forth. . . .

Overall, the Chinese in Southeast Asia should not be called 'Overseas Chinese' as it is a label, which is appropriate only for citizens of China living overseas.

(Tan 1997: 25, 29)

Statements like these add a question mark to the basic theoretical construction behind diasporic thinking, especially the triangular structure of migrant, host and home. For example, if a host country is a de facto home country, and if the migrant is a citizen of that home country, where does that leave the diasporic notion of home country? It even questions whether ethnic Chinese in Southeast Asia can be considered diasporic or belonging to a diasporic community. For example, the Sino-Indonesian Treaty on Dual Nationality, signed in Bandung on 22 April 1955, at first glance seems to lend support to the existence of a Chinese diaspora in the region. This treaty stated that ethnic Chinese had to choose which nationality they preferred, Indonesian or Chinese, during the period from January 1960 to January 1962. Most of the about one million ethnic Chinese with dual nationality registered, and out of those, about 65 per cent opted for Indonesian citizenship whereas the rest went 'back' to China (Tan Chee Beng 1997).

The question is whether these returning migrants really opted for a new life in China now that political events beyond their control had taken a different turn. It seems to me, after having read James Chin Kong's (2003) article on returned 'overseas' Chinese in Hong Kong, that this 'repatriation' was a decision forced upon them. Many of these people originally moved from Indonesia to China because of discrimination in the 1950s and early 1960s. The 'home' country, in this case China, did not, however, treat the returning (Indonesian) Chinese well. In fact, the discrimination that the Indonesian Chinese fled from was now carried out by their 'real' compatriots. Many of the returnees then moved on to Hong Kong in the late 1960s and early 1970s only to find out that they could not return to what they thought of as their real homeland, namely Indonesia, the nation they migrated from in the first place. Their China passport had made them a security liability there. They had to stay in Hong Kong and were thus stuck in between two 'homelands'.

4.2 The notion of contemporary Chinese-ness in Southeast Asia

Empirical evidence like this adds an even more serious question mark to the theoretical extrapolations, this time in relation to diasporic movements, and thus prompts us to test the outer limits of diasporic identities. Echoing the argument that ethnic Chinese networks and diaspora are not necessarily coherent and inter-related, Ien Ang (2001) voices a warning note. She writes:

[W]hile the transnationalism of diasporas is often taken as an implicit point of critique of the territorial boundedness and the internally homogenising perspective of the nation state, the limits of diaspora lie precisely in its own assumed boundedness, its inevitable tendency to stress its internal coherence and unity, logically set apart from 'others'. Ultimately, diaspora is a concept of sameness-in-dispersal, not of togetherness-in-difference.

(Ang 2001: 12–13)

Here Ang concurs with the critique forwarded by Tan, namely that the ethnic Chinese are not alike even though they are of Chinese descent somewhere along the line. Like any other ethnic group, they try to adapt to the community in which they are residing, thus becoming more or less integrated there. Playing on the definition of diaspora as literally meaning 'the scattering of seeds', Ang defines diasporic networks as producing subjects for whom notions of identity and belonging are unsettled. A dominant tendency, she continues, in thinking about the Chinese diaspora is to suppress the ways diasporic identities are produced through creolisation and hybridisation in favour of a hierarchical centring and a linear rerouting back to an imagined ancestral home.

Such a decentred conception of diaspora, in which the constitution of identity is based on creolisation, positions cultural interaction and identification in the field of social engineering and political strategy. For example, playing on the interaction between achieved and ascribed identity and adding a time dimension of about one or two generations for allowing you as an ethnic Chinese to internalise the various practices of your community of residence, it is tempting to say you are what you are expected to be, a contextually determined individual, reflecting your current relationship towards your country of residence. Consequently, having an identity as an ethnic Chinese in Malaysia does not necessarily imply that you are affiliated with China or devoted to Chinese culture and traditions. On the contrary, you are a Malaysian of Chinese descent and, for the time being, you have deposited your social and political loyalty in the local powers that be.[3]

By accepting such a perspective we see that a transnationally related identity is not a result of diasporic movements or a nationalist ideological interpretation of 'overseas Chinese' as in the case of China, but rather a bottom-up initiated perception of identity-making in a potentially hostile community of residence. Adherence to a transnational identity thus depends on domestic sociopolitical events and developments.

Going further into this reveals that the construction of a Southeast Asian ethnic Chinese is a combination of ascribed and negotiated elements, which combined make up a locally specific understanding of Chinese identity. An ethnic Chinese identity is thus ascribed by and negotiated with the 'dominant other'. Such a construction of Chinese-ness in collaboration with someone's local community of residence makes a Chinese a Malaysian or whatever Southeast Asian citizen of Chinese descent. Ang's own personal history is a strong case in point. A crack in such constructions occur when specific social and political events expose faultlines between various ethnic groups otherwise thought of as 'completely' assimilated. This defines some of them as *bumiputra* or *pribumis* while others are identified as localised permanent residents or citizens of Chinese descent somewhere down the line, and are thus 'othered' in the process. Conceptions of belonging therefore fluctuate according to local social and political conditions instead of affective-expressive components, as Shuval would have it.

In an interesting article, 'Who Wants to Be Diasporic?', Allen Chun (2003) writes that one can see the conceptual limitations and the sociological relevance of the term *diaspora* in that it only applies to particular contexts. The concept of diaspora not only invokes the existence of social margins and alienated communities. It also defends values of marginality in challenging the hegemony of the centre to speak on behalf of dispossessed 'others' (Chun 2003: 2–3).

Chun continues by arguing that over time, however, increasing numbers of Chinese have become assimilated or creolised into their communities of residence, such as the *peranakans* in Malaysia, but this fact simply accentuates the polarisation of the ethnic Chinese population in contrast to other ethnic groups. In fact, their separateness is not just a function of ethnic differences but also of their status as, say, businesspeople operating in tightly controlled personal networks. The applicability of the term *diaspora* to characterise the ethnic Chinese in Southeast Asia, even in the pre-modern era, is therefore debatable.

In Chun's words, the history of diaspora reveals in the final analysis not a primordial semantic meaning of the term so much as the restrictions imposed on its use by its underlying sociopolitical context. The latter is the most important one. A case in point concerns the currently changing use of the term 'overseas Chinese'. In the pre-modern, pre-national period, Chinese sojourners in Southeast Asia were less citizens of a unified polity than disparate dialect groups tied together by kin ties and attachments to a provincial homeland. As Wang Gungwu once noted, 'the Chinese never had a concept of identity, only a concept of Chinese-ness, of being Chinese and of becoming un-Chinese' (Wang 1989).

During the pre-modern era, the multicultural skills of Chinese merchants were less a function of their multiple identities than strategic considerations based on occupational and political necessity. Success in social intercourse and economic exchange demanded fluency in many dialects and languages as well as familiarity with diverse customs. Wang phrases this pragmatism in the following way: '[F]or most of these merchants and entrepreneurs, being Chinese had nothing to do with becoming closer to China. It was a private and domestic matter (that) only manifested (itself) when needed to strengthen a business contact or to follow an approved public convention' (Wang 1991: 139).

Finally, Chun (2003) maintains that much of the success that ethnic Chinese entrepreneurs have experienced in Southeast Asia has been achieved through multicultural skills, often by downplaying ethnic difference through processes of assimilation. In the political realm, co-optation and networking have been staple norms of social mobility strategies by the ethnic Chinese, even if this results in cultural assimilation. As such, the maintenance of ethnic identity and lifestyles is irrelevant or secondary to these politico-economic concerns (Chun 2003: 8–9).

Insightful though these extrapolations may be, just like Ang, I am nonetheless sceptical of the use of the concept of assimilation. If one, for example, takes this concept to its ultimate limit, this would lead to the assumption that ethnically distinctive features will become hybridised to such an extent that the original ethnic identities involved are gradually being dissolved and a new set of commonly agreed upon cultural denominators will take over as identity markers. Such a perspective can only be deceptive. To my understanding, processes of assimilation or hybridity always rest on a foundation of asymmetrical inter-ethnic power relationships.

For example, in the case of the Manadonese Chinese and the Minahasa, the dominant ethnic group in North Sulawesi, Indonesia, it would be absurd to imagine that the latter would give an inch in their perception of ethnic supremacy in relation to the Chinese, even though both parties claim to be totally assimilated, especially the Chinese. However, processes of assimilation can only be a means to an end and never an end product in themselves. In my view, claims of inter-ethnic assimilation are a subtle way of stipulating power relations that are basically manifested in social integration and a more or less peaceful co-existence. Beneath the rhetoric of assimilation, ethnic distinctions remain but they have descended to a lower level of social practice. Seen from a positive perspective, they resurface during ceremonial occasions, which are socially acceptable to the dominant 'other', for example, the Chinese New Year (*Imlek*) and the Chinese lion dance; from a negative perspective they re-boot otherwise dormant sociopolitical fault-lines that tend to draw up problematic ethnic classifications, thus instigating inter-ethnic social and political tensions (Jakobsen 2004a).

Returning to the essence of Chun's (2003) discussion, namely that classical diasporic thinking is an outdated mode of understanding the relationship between transnationalism and localism and should be replaced by what he calls 'situatedness', a closer look at network practices among ethnic Chinese, especially in a historical perspective, reinforces his point. The tendency in network practices seems to go towards greater complexity over time, whereby the grounded 'situatedness' of the individual actor in relation to network formation gradually becomes more important than transnational ethnic-affiliated networks.

Lau-Fong Mak and I-Chun Kung (1999) distinguish, historically speaking, between two main types of Southeast Asian Chinese networks: primary ethnic Chinese networks and secondary and achieving networks. Primary ethnic Chinese networks were groups consisting of ethnic Chinese who spoke a creolised language and who practised a distinctly marginalised subculture during the eighteenth and nineteenth centuries. Such networks were furthermore determined by occupation. In Singapore, for example, businesses related to commerce, international trading, finance and manufacturing were closely associated with Hokkien speakers, whereas the Hakka and Cantonese were mainly engaged in carpentry, smithing and herbal medicine. The Hainanese were mostly attracted to service-oriented occupations, while the Henghwa and Hochchia groups dominated transportation-related businesses. Finally, the Teochiu group was more inclined towards primary production activities such as planting, poultry rearing and fishing (Mak and Kung 1999). According to Mak and Kung, occupation and speech recognition suggest rigid social systems. A closed immigrant community usually constitutes dense networks, which provide the new immigrants with critical resources such as training, financial support, job contacts, supply of labour and information. Many early

Chinese migrants in Southeast Asia depended on these forms of networks to make a living.

In the 1950s and 1960s, these types of networks began to lose prominence throughout Southeast Asia. As a result, the earlier Chinese business networks based on speech origin gradually became less universal or prevalent. In Singapore and Peninsular Malaysia, for example, such networks are showing signs of eclipse, although neighbouring countries such as Indonesia and the Philippines might retain some of them (Mak and Kung 1999: 4–5, 9).

Secondary and achieving networks connect individuals who share certain experiences, status and resources. Club memberships, religious affiliations and alumni groups are some of the common criteria for forming social and business networks. Of these, alumni or classmates are a more vital and common source of social embeddedness and thus more conducive to networking practices. These kinds of networks have spread all over Southeast Asia with a sharp concentration in Malaysia, Indonesia, Singapore, Thailand and the Philippines.

Finally, according to Mak and Kung, the latest development within the secondary network category is that it does not necessarily draw on ascribed traits or anything specifically Chinese, but rather on business and professional affiliations. Among ethnic Chinese, especially in Malaysia, this kind of network consists primarily of the English-educated or the racially protected professional groups. They do feel a certain degree of commonality, but it is not as strong as the 'underdog feeling' experienced by the Chinese-educated. Mak and Kung are referring in particular to the affirmative action policy in Malaysia as producing this perception of an 'underdog feeling'. If a difference has to be made between the English- and the Chinese-educated groups of ethnic Chinese entrepreneurs, the former could be labelled the power elite and the latter the economic elite. As long as globalisation remains the mainstream avenue of business development, members of the English-educated network will continue to occupy the apex of power, politically as well as economically. Furthermore, as long as networks continue to be bifurcated between various streams of education, tensions between the economic and power elites will continue and further diversify the ethnic Chinese community within the region (Mak and Kung 1999: 7–9, 15).

4.3   Grounded cosmopolitanism among Southeast Asian ethnic Chinese

When comparing the statements made by Ang, Tan, Wang, Chun and Mak and Kung to my own research on the ethnic Chinese entrepreneurs in both Manado, North Sulawesi, Indonesia, and among Chinese entrepreneurs in Penang, Malaysia, all seem to agree that the theoretical parameters behind studies of the relationship between adherence to a diaspora, processes of identity formation, and questions of (ethnic) belonging are in for a critical overhaul. As an initial step in this direction I would like to point to a renewed interest in the concept of cosmopolitanism (Breckenridge *et al.* 2002; Vertovec and Cohen 2002), especially the version of this concept that has been termed 'grounded cosmopolitanism'.

On 29 April 2004, the Asia Research Institute at the National University of Singapore held a workshop on 'Identities, Nations and Cosmopolitan Practice: Interrogating the Work of Pnina and Richard Werbner'. One of the outcomes of this workshop was a volume based on the proceedings on the topic of 'Ethnicities, Diaspora and "Grounded" Cosmopolitanisms in Asia'. This is an interesting volume, as it touches on some of the ways notions of diaspora and cosmopolitanism can be re-conceptualised.

In the introduction to the volume, Joel S. Kahn advocates a re-evaluation of this rather antiquated concept. He writes:

> Although some may continue to advocate . . . the notion of the 'cosmopolitan' as a rootless, identity-less 'citizen of the world' – of the kind favoured by (Emmanuel) Kant, there has been a growing awareness of the importance of other models of cosmopolitan practice. These are based on a rather different view of cosmopolitanism as fixed in circumstances that are unique and contingent, and cosmopolitans as inevitably embedded in particularistic cultural circumstances.
>
> (Kahn 2004: 3)

Kahn ascribes the honour of introducing this 'anthropological' version of cosmopolitan practice to Pnina and Richard Werbner, thus embedding it in recent social and political theory. This is, however, not about importing Western universalising models into an Asian context. On the contrary, according to Kahn, there have been and still are local or regional cosmopolitan models in Asia to be recovered. He goes on to argue that Southeast Asia has, diachronically speaking, always been one of the most cosmopolitan regions in the world due to it being the gateway to the East and the West respectively (Kahn 2004: 3).

These insights are very important when discussing decentred diasporas in relation to the ethnic Chinese in Southeast Asia. First of all, it reinforces the critical approaches towards diasporic theory as forwarded by Ang, Tan, and Chun in that such theories need to be grounded in local social and political circumstances if they are to have any explanatory power beyond mere theoretical extrapolations. Thus, instead of looking for diasporic affiliations such as those advocated by Shuval and colleagues, a conception of grounded cosmopolitanism would be more conducive when discussing transnational movements among ethnic Chinese (entrepreneurs) in Southeast Asia. The logic behind this is that one can move around nationally as well as internationally without losing one's sense of belonging, whether it is grounded in terms of ethnicity or citizenship in one's community of residence. The classical diasporic perception of a homeland, however illusive it might be, presupposes a static, harmonious and happy society that is capable of comforting the more or less voluntarily 'exiled'. As such this can only be an illusion. For example, how many Malaysians of Chinese descent regard China as their father- or motherland? They might like to do business there or visit as tourists, but to settle there permanently is not on their agenda. It is such deceptive perceptions of a 'homeland' that this chapter has sought to debunk when putting forward the alternative notion of grounded cosmopolitanism.

Similarly, the diasporic perception of 'host' community or country is equally a misfit when discussing Southeast Asian ethnic Chinese and their perceptions of belonging. As Tan stressed, it is an offence to address an ethnic Chinese as an 'overseas Chinese', as the country in which he or she resides is his or her home. Ethnic Chinese in Southeast Asia are thus neither migrants nor sojourners to this region. They are at home in their respective countries of residence. This also excludes the final element of the diasporic triangle of migrant, home and host, when discussing Southeast Asian ethnic Chinese, namely the status as migrant. A migrant then is thus a person who moves regularly in order to find work or, I would add, moves from one country, place or locality to another. As we have seen in this chapter, this is not the case for the ethnic Chinese in Southeast Asia. They do not move around looking for jobs. Nor do they move around on a regular basis. They are citizens of their country of residence where they have their business, even though this business might have been transnationalised to a certain extent; however, that does not make them diasporic. On this basis, the only logical conclusion is that current diasporic theory cannot be applied to ethnic Chinese in this region, as Southeast Asian Chinese do not fulfil any of the three main parameters of that theory.

Consequently, the concept of grounded cosmopolitanism is thus much more appealing when studying ethnic Chinese in general, ethnic Chinese entrepreneurs and Chinese business networking in Southeast Asia. As I have also argued in this chapter, the social and political circumstances surrounding ethnic Chinese entrepreneurs and their enterprises in this region is of paramount importance when assessing whether a business is viable or not. In case the local social and political environment is not conducive for doing business, then one has to engage in negotiating an acceptable solution with pertinent representatives from one's community of residence, thus creating a way for one's business to melt into the entrepreneurial landscape of that community. This produces a sense of social and political security, however flimsy and precarious.

In case the social, political or economic situation in one's community of residence threatens otherwise more or less harmonious inter-ethnic relations, as the Chinese in Indonesia experienced during the fall of Suharto in May 1998, then the international community, and the Southeast Asian region in particular, constitutes a temporary safe haven. Not, however, in the form of pushing the Malaysian citizens of Chinese descent towards a Chinese father- or motherland, as indicated by conventional diasporic theory, but rather towards providing the temporary refugee with options that are helpful to his or her current situation, along ethnic lines or otherwise. In the Indonesian case, many Chinese moved or fled to Singapore, Malaysia or Hong Kong during the 1998 incident to monitor the situation with an eye on returning to Indonesia at a later and safer date. During such crises there is no doubt about notions of belonging. The father- or motherland was to them Indonesia, not China or anywhere else. The country of refuge was a temporary one that allowed the refugees to maintain their perception of Indonesian identity. Such events show the explanatory capabilities of the concept of grounded cosmopolitanism.

Combining the two, the international and the local, implies that it is possible to be simultaneously cosmopolitan and local, or as Kahn (2004) formulates it, both communalistic and open to otherness simultaneously. As such, the notion of grounded cosmopolitanism relates very well to the other key idea forwarded in this book, namely glocalisation, which also demonstrates that it is not possible to disentangle the global from the local and vice versa. The point in this context is that an ethnic Chinese is not an entrepreneurial sojourner filled with longing for a Chinese homeland. An ethnic Chinese is an individual who is grounded in a specific locality that he or she calls home. The primordial longing that is simmering behind the notion of a Chinese diaspora is thus not on the agenda when talking about grounded cosmopolitanism. On the contrary, home is where you are, that is, where you have decided it to be, and your community of residence accepts that decision. As such, your identity is a flexible mixture of ascribed, constructed and negotiated elements that perfectly fits the conditions of an increasingly complex, diversifying and interrelated world.

Having linked grounded cosmopolitanism with the concept of glocalisation as discussed in Chapter 1, and then discussed the complexities of the Southeast Asian Chinese mind-set and the context in which it has been and still is being moulded, the following chapter takes a closer look at how the ethnic Chinese in Malaysia negotiate their particular niche in the contemporary multicultural societal Malaysian environment. As discussed, notions of Chinese-ness and being an ethnic Chinese must be put into a local dynamic context, where specific opportunities and constraints constitute the forces that provide the overall framework for being Chinese in a Malaysian context.

Notes

1 *Guanxi* constitutes a form of social exchange based on sentiments and emotions and is marked by a mutual belief in reciprocity and loyalty.
2 Riggs (2001). I owe this particular insight to Arif Dirlik, personal communication, September 2004.
3 I have discussed the fluidity and thus political expediency of ethnic identity extensively in Jakobsen (2002) and (2004a, 2004b).

Part III
The local context

5 'Divided thou shall be'

Understanding ethnic divisions in Malaysia

5.1 The relationship between Malays and Chinese according to Mahathir

One way to quickly get deeper insight into how the relationship between the ethnic Chinese and Malays in Malaysian society is played out is to study the memoirs of prominent Malays. A good example of this is to read the memoirs of Mahathir Mohamad, who for twenty-two years served Malaysia as prime minister. Many articles and books have been written about Mahathir and his many encounters on both the domestic and international political scenes. They have, however, generally taken an etic perspective, that is, an outsider perspective, when portraying the politician and/or the private person. Memoirs, on the other hand, provide the reader with an emic perspective, as the person who is writing the book is also the person in question.

A Doctor in the House. The Memoirs of Tun Dr Mahathir Mohamad, published in 2011, is indeed an interesting account of Mahathir's life, not only his professional life, but from the very outset, beginning with his birth on 10 July 1925, continuing with his years as prime minister, beginning on 27 June 1981, and ending with Tun Abdullah Ahmad Badawi's swearing-in ceremony as his successor as prime minister of Malaysia on 31 October 2003. One of the main themes in the book is the relationship between the three main ethnic groups in Malaysia – the Malays, the Chinese and the Indians – and the impact this inter-ethnic constellation has had on national cohesion.

The title of the book, *A Doctor in the House,* is very well chosen. First of all, Mahathir *is* a doctor by profession and by playing on this, Malaysia becomes a patient in need of a doctor when he took over as prime minister. The book does not hide the fact that Mahathir is a staunch Malay, who is very concerned about his fellow Malays. Besides describing his fascinating life story and career, he focuses on the problem Malaysia has been dealing with ever since independence in 1957, a problem that basically has its roots back in colonial times, namely the relationship between the Malays, the Chinese and the Indians who together constitute the nation's three main ethnic groups.

Mahathir laments the fate of the Malays compared especially to the Chinese. The original rulers of the Malay territory, the Malays were forced to accept the

British colonisers, who then introduced the Chinese as a kind of buffer between themselves and the Malay sultans. The Chinese grew from societal underdogs to become a strong economic force, marginalising the Malays in the process. Mahathir's main political project throughout his career was to reverse this situation by restoring them to what he perceived to be the previous glory of the Malays. This was to be done, according to his understanding, not at the expense of the Chinese or Indians, but by reinstalling the Malays in their rightful position in Malaysian society, lifting them out of a self-imposed perception of being poor, backward and not respected in their own country.

His biggest concern in this context was the mind-set of the Malays. Not the one developed during the British era but rather the original indigenous mind-set that was one of politeness, restraint and softness, according to Mahathir. These qualities, noble as they are, do not match the aggressiveness of the Chinese, who have been accustomed to fighting for their very existence because of their precarious social position. Thus, the Chinese have developed a mind-set of entrepreneurship and robustness that has carried them forward to their present, according to Mahathir, dominant ethnic position in the Malaysian society, thus relegating the majority Malays to an inferior societal position, a position reinforced by the original Malay mind-set. The Malays must therefore reinvent themselves to regain their rightful position in society. This was the main project that Mahathir tried hard to promote all through his political career, a project that made him a Malay chauvinist in the eyes of his opponents.

After the violent racial riots in Kuala Lumpur on 13 May 1969, where Malays and Chinese fought each other in deadly encounters, remedies were introduced. One of the main themes of the New Economic Policy (NEP), initiated in 1971, was to narrow the socio-economic gap between the Malays and the two other ethnic groups, especially the Chinese. Under the NEP, the Industrial Act of 1975 required that non-Malay-owned companies allocate 30 per cent of their shares or equity to ethnic Malays to engage them in business. This policy, framed in an affirmative action programme, was not confined to the economic realm but included the education sector, where a quota system for Malay students in government universities was imposed, thus providing them with better access to higher education compared to the other two ethnic groups. As a consequence, a massive, mainly Chinese-led brain drain and capital drain took place, the effects of which Malaysia is still suffering from.[1]

To Mahathir's disappointment, the affirmative action programme did not deliver as expected. On the contrary, the protection and privileges bestowed on the Malays by the NEP weakened them further by lulling the next generation into complacency, thinking that the NEP's affirmative action programme would always be there for them to fall back on. According to Mahathir, the Malays like the easy way out and thus failed to rise above the challenges. They stopped trying to adapt to changing circumstances and remained laid-back and compliant. This is perhaps the biggest failure during the entire Mahathir era. According to observers, its main ramification, the inter-ethnic stalemate, unfortunately constitutes a kind of 'lid' on the economic development of Malaysia.[2]

5.2 Looking beyond Mahathir: the wider political and economic ramifications of the inter-ethnic deadlock

Looking back to Figure 3.1, which delineated enablers and strategic reform initiatives in the NEM introduced in 2009, informants have insisted that economic deregulation as spelled out in the NEM is fine, but the model was still perceived as retaining the inter-ethnic 'lid' on economic performance. By this is meant that the affirmative action policy that was introduced in 1971 as part of the NEP was still very much enforced. The informants are referring to point 5 in particular in the NEM under the section 'Strategic Reform Initiatives', labelled 'Transparent and Market Friendly Affirmative Action'. According to the informants, the question is how 'market friendly' an affirmative action policy can be, given that it is based on preferential treatment of Malays at the expense of the Chinese and Indians. If the market is to be truly open, then it has to respect the first pillar in the overall national reform scheme, namely '1Malaysia', introduced by Prime Minister Najib on 16 September 2010, which sends a strong political signal for equal access for all Malaysians regardless of ethnic belonging.[3]

Why is the affirmative action policy maintained in the NEM? To explain this one has to look at the economic policies behind the NEP and the underlying inter-ethnic policy dimension embedded in it. Khoo Boo Teik writes that without dismissing some of the NEP's more generalised underlying principles about an equitable inter-ethnic distribution of wealth via affirmative action programmes, he suggests that the NEP was never restricted exclusively to ethnicity and ethnic relations. The NEP encompassed federal policies that affected ethnic identities, inter-ethnic power sharing and an ethnically targeted distribution of developmental benefits, but was not confined to these issues (Khoo 2004: 4).

Khoo concludes that the NEP could heighten as well as diminish ethnic differences to the extent that issues of ethnic identity and problems of cultural grievances had an economic aspect to them. The main goal of the NEP's socio-economic policies was to diminish the likelihood of intense ethnic economic rivalry, as the Mahathir government's economic solutions to cultural problems in the 1990s encouraged a deeper sense of national purpose and identity (Khoo 2004: 18).

Looking at the political realm, however, one finds several examples of a discourse on tense inter-ethnic relations. For example, during 2006, several complaints were voiced on behalf of the Malay community in Penang that they were being marginalised in terms of political influence because the Chinese-dominated political party Gerakan, a part of the ruling coalition *Barisan Nasional* (BN), has held the position of chief minister in Penang since 1969. This critique of not contributing to racial harmony in Penang was rejected by the party's vice president, Datuk' Teng Hock Nam. He said that such statements are not fair just by looking at the racial makeup of its members. Although about 80 per cent of Gerakan members are Chinese, the party has always adopted a non-racial approach to Malaysian politics.

Racial tensions are still occasionally surfacing thus bringing evidence of constantly simmering strife just beneath an otherwise tranquil multiracial surface.

One only needs to read newspaper articles in the *Straits Times* in late November 2007 on Malaysian Chinese who immigrated to other countries for a better life and job opportunities there compared to those found in Malaysia, as well as the articles on Malaysian Indian demonstrations in November and early December 2007. That the inter-ethnic question was still not solved in 2009 could be seen in a July article in the *Straits Times,* where the former prime minister, Mahathir Mohamad, maintained that non-Malays are the real masters in Malaysia. Mahathir was quoted as saying that the affirmative action share of the Malaysian corporate community is only 20 per cent, while Chinese Malaysians hold 50 per cent, despite making up only 26 per cent of the population. On 23 May 2011 *Pertubuhan Pribumi Perkasa Malaysia* (Perkasa)[4] emerged in the aftermath of the March 2008 general election, when UMNO's hold on power was threatened by the loss of a substantial number of Malay votes to the opposition. Perkasa became the answer to the Malays' search for a new entity to represent them, increasing racial tensions in many parts of Malaysia. On the basis of this, I argue that the affirmative action policy is still very much in existence. The deep impact this policy has had on Chinese-owned SMEs' efforts to move up the value chain, and the damage it has done to the overall development of the Malaysian economy, will be discussed in greater detail in Chapter 6.

5.3   Transforming the national political economy: the latest developments on the affirmative action policy

According to Izatun Shari from *The Star* newspaper,[5] Prime Minister Najib explained on 1 July 2009 that the policy changes behind the NEM had to be made because of the drastic changes in the global economic scenario since the inception of the NEP and the failure of the Foreign Investment Committee (FIC) to produce the desired result of increasing *bumiputra* equity in the Malaysian business community. According to Najib, the FIC, as an instrument, has not produced the desired results over the past nineteen years. *Bumiputra* participation in business has remained stagnant during that time. In the *New Straits Times* on 3 August 2009, Najib was quoted as saying that *bumiputra* equity shareholding since the inception of the NEP in 1971 seems to be stuck at 18 or 19 per cent in 2009. He continues: 'We need to have a new instrument but it has to be more market friendly. In the process, we are embarking on a new philosophy which will help the best and good bumiputras in business, not just any bumiputra, who are willing to help themselves'.

On eliminating the 30 per cent quota for companies seeking listing, Najib said investors were dissatisfied with such a condition. He pointed out that even the allotment of shares by the FIC to *bumiputras* in the past did not work as most of them would 'straight away sell-down an enormous amount'. He continued: 'We have done our research. Very little shares are still left. The old model is not sustainable. Of the RM54bil in shares allocated, only RM2bil worth of shares are left in the hands of bumiputras. That's a D-minus performance'.

The federal government has announced a series of measures, including dropping *bumiputra* equity requirements for new initial public offerings, and created fund management firms to boost international investment in Malaysia. In announcing these measures at the 'Invest Malaysia' business fair on 30 June 2009, Najib said the FIC's 30 per cent *bumiputra* equity requirement for firms seeking a listing in Malaysia had been dropped but these companies were now required to offer 50 per cent of the public shareholding spread to *bumiputra* investors. 'The 30% requirement remains but it is a macro objective', Najib was recorded as saying.[6]

With immediate effect, FIC guidelines covering the acquisition of equity stakes, mergers and takeovers were also repealed. The FIC will no longer process share transactions or impose equity conditions on such transactions. Furthermore, it will no longer process property transactions, except where it involves the dilution of *bumiputra* or government interests for properties valued at RM20mil and higher. 'In the context of the challenges that the nation faces, the guidelines of the FIC appear to have outlived their usefulness', Najib said and continued, 'When the FIC was first introduced in 1974, it represented a major component of the strategy for growth with equity. Today, it is no longer an effective instrument to support growth with equity'.

In the 1970s, *bumiputra* equity was only 2.4 per cent. 'Given the very low base, it was perhaps relevant to adopt allocation type policies to quickly redress the imbalance', Najib was quoted as saying. 'Today, we face a completely different scenario. Investment policies creating regulatory uncertainty and that are not in line with international practice will only constrain our growth potential', he continued. The pursuit of sustainable equity required a focus on effective and meaningful economic participation, not just ownership. Further, it has been shown that the lack of capital results in the 30 per cent stake held at the company level was not sustainable, according to Shari.

Prime Minister Najib further announced in his speech on 30 June 2009 that ownership in the wholesale segment of the fund management industry had been fully liberalised to allow for 100 per cent ownership for qualified companies to set up operations locally. However, he said national interest in terms of strategic sectors would continue to be safeguarded through sector regulators such as the Energy Commission, Commercial Vehicles Licensing Board, National Water Services Commission and Malaysian Communications and Multimedia Commission. The foreign shareholding limits for unit trust management companies was also raised to 70 per cent, from 49 per cent.

He then announced the establishment of a new institution, Ekuiti Nasional Bhd (Ekuinas), aimed at making investments in new and high-growth sectors. It would invest jointly with private sector funds to promote genuine partnerships and a fully commercial approach. 'In this way, the participation of bumiputras through Ekuinas will be premised on merit', Najib said. 'With the comprehensive easing of FIC guidelines at the firm level, the Economic Planning Unit will re-focus its efforts towards co-ordinating and monitoring distributional policies at a macro level', he added.

Ekuinas was to be established with an initial capital of RM 500 million and eventually enlarged to RM 10 billion, and would invest in high-growth sectors, including education, medical tourism, education tourism, information and communications technology and oil and gas, Minister Tan Sri Nor Mohamed Yakcop said at 'Invest Malaysia 2009'. Ekuinas would begin operations 'soon, meaning this year, not next year'.

While Ekuinas might jointly invest in projects with non-*bumiputra* partners, there would be a specific *bumiputra* agenda, Nor Mohamed said. He emphasised that Ekuinas aimed to be meritocratic and improve *bumiputra* participation in the economy by supporting capable *bumiputra* entrepreneurs without detriment to any other ethnic groups in the country. 'It is a win-win situation; we are acting so that no group is disincentivised or a hindrance to anyone', he said, adding that while Ekuinas would report to the government it would not be run like a government department but by professional staff operating outside the government. Meanwhile, the Economic Planning Unit (EPU)[7] said that Ekuinas would jointly invest with the private sector, reflecting a genuine partnership and, through a fully commercial approach, would ensure meritocracy of participating *bumiputras*.

While the government remains committed to the goals of equitable growth, its approach will be to implement these goals in a market-friendly manner, given that robust and sustainable growth is a pre-condition for equitable distribution. On 19 June 2009, Najib said that RM 9 billion worth of projects had been awarded under the government's RM 67 billion stimulus packages to stimulate economic growth. Of this, RM 3 billion has so far been paid out. 'Given the step-up progressive payments to be made as these projects are rolled out, I am confident that this spending injection into the domestic economy and the related multiplier effects will help cushion the impact of the sharp external downturn and set the stage for economic recovery in the second half of this year,' he said.

On whether Ekuinas was established to achieve the 30 per cent *bumiputra* quota target, he said, 'It is not the only way. There are other ways as well to achieve the 30% bumiputra equity. It is important to see that the 1Malaysia concept is translated in the economic sense'. To a question on whether he was confident that the *Ali Baba* practice, a practice where *bumiputra* participation in business is in name only while non-*bumiputras* run the actual business, would be eliminated with the policy reform, Najib replied, 'I don't think you can eliminate sleeping partners overnight but you will reduce it substantially. We are helping those who want to help themselves'.

The latest development on the affirmative action policy was recorded on 19 March 2012. The newspaper *The Star* quoted Najib as saying that contracts awarded to *bumiputras* must be based on an individual's expertise and not anything else. He continues by saying that there have been weaknesses in the *bumiputra* community in the past. It was not the people's fault but the corporate figure that lacked knowledge in running an organisation. 'The government had', he said, 'to pump in a huge amount of money to bail out these companies. So to avoid this, contracts should be awarded to *bumiputra* based on merit and expertise'.[8]

5.4 Where to go from here?

One of the major challenges to the political and economic stability of Malaysia is the affirmative action policy, as also identified in the institutional analysis in Chapter 3. The political establishment headed by Prime Minister Najib is very well aware of that and tries through the NEM to neutralise some of the most negative ramifications of it. The question is, though, whether this task is possible, taking the current political environment into account. It remains to be seen whether Najib can roll back or modify the current affirmative action scheme and instead introduce a system based on meritocracy combined with a *bumiputra* aid system to help those Malays who have the capacity to engage themselves in business.

Employing an institutional theoretical perspective on this, that is, whether Najib is capable of changing the affirmative action policy prompts another important query to surface. According to Chan Huan Chiang from the Penang Institute, Najib can say whatever he likes as long as it does not upset the institutional framework within which he is working.[9] To put it in another way, the prime minister can say anything he likes as long as it is sanctioned by the political institutional framework, especially UMNO, and more generally BN.

Here it is important to make a reference to the difference in speed between what is being said in a political discourse and how fast results of such a discourse can be implemented within an institutional framework. The main question being asked here, I guess, is whether a politician has the capability to act on his or her own behalf thereby changing reality overnight. As I see it, it is rather difficult to implement major changes based on individual preferences because of the various kinds of stakeholders that make up the institutional framework. This crucial distinction in terms of speed and capability of implementing change has a great impact on the content and direction of the political process. In order to probe further into the distinction between political rhetoric and institutional inertness, we have to distinguish between two different yet interrelated kinds of institutional frameworks in a Malaysian context. The first one consists of the political platforms of UMNO and BN. As they constitute the political establishment currently in power, they also define the overall political framework within which the prime minister has to perform. Because of stakeholder interest in this context, arguments and personal political positioning that deviate from this framework do not have much chance of being implemented.

The second institutional framework is made up of the politically motivated economic stakeholders that back up UMNO and BN policies, as they constitute a kind of economic carrying capacity behind the overall policy being implemented. These individuals are the ones who have benefitted the most from the affirmative action policy. We are not talking about the ordinary voters who support the policies of UMNO and BN, but rather a minority, perhaps the 18 to 19 per cent that Najib alluded to who have benefitted from the policy. On the basis of this they are the ones who have a direct or indirect influence on which direction the current federal government develops the Malaysian economy and society.[10]

The approximately 80 per cent of the supporters of the UMNO and BN policies are not the ones who get shares in relation to the 30 per cent equity scheme, as they live and work outside the industrial arrangement that this scheme feeds into. They are mainly farmers, petty traders and micro entrepreneurs. The approximately 20 per cent that has a direct interest in this scheme are either already major industrialists who have the political connections that propel them into the scheme, or major interest groups that have the capacity to influence major sections within the 80 per cent. In particular these are religious groups that have their own more or less hidden agenda. Those two major groupings within the 20 per cent are the ones who would lose out in case the affirmative action policy were to be rolled back. These are the stakeholders who constitute the second institutional framework.

It is thus the combined efforts of these two institutional frameworks that determine how far Najib can go when discussing major changes to the affirmative action policies or any other areas for that matter that are of vital interest to these frameworks. The degree of inertness of these frameworks is thus proportional to the interest of the various stakeholders who govern the informal part of it, thus maintaining a kind of status quo of the established societal institutional framework.

In the following chapter the political and economic ramifications of the affirmative action policy on the ethnic Chinese- and Indian-owned SMEs in Penang will be discussed. After describing this particular SME community in relation to the overall industrial environment in Penang, a discussion of the mind-set of the ethnic Chinese and Indian owners of these SMEs follows to assess in what way the societal factors just described have impacted this group of entrepreneurs. Three case studies of ethnic Chinese- and Indian-owned companies are then discussed to get a glimpse of the harsh reality behind this race-based policy governing the performative level of the national and regional economy.

Notes

1 A direct consequence of this academic brain drain is a lower academic level of the remaining students that has resulted in an increasing gap between what the universities can provide in terms of quality students and what both the local and international industries need. For further comments on the relationship between university graduates and the industry, see *The Star,* 5 March 2012. Accessed 5 March 2012. For further discussions on the Malaysian brain drain see Chapter 7.
2 I return to this 'lid' in Chapter 6.
3 For details see the official Web site of 1Malaysia: www.1malaysia.com.my/my/.
4 Pertubuhan Pribumi Perkasa Malaysia or Perkasa is a non-governmental Malay supremacy organisation that was formed by Ibrahim Ali in the aftermath of the Malaysian general elections in 2008. This conservative, extreme-right ethnic Malay organisation is led by its president, Ibrahim Ali, with Mahathir Mohamad, the former prime minister, as advisor.
5 The following discussion is based on news clips from *The Star,* 1 July 2009, written by Izatun Shari. Accessed 7 March 2010.

6 For the speech in full, see www.treasury.gov.my/pdf/ucapan/investmalaysia.pdf.
7 For details on the EPU, see www.epu.gov.my/en/home.
8 *The Star,* 19 March 2012. Accessed 24 March 2012.
9 Personal communication, 6 March 2012.
10 I owe this insight to Toh Kin Woon, Penang Institute. Personal communication, 22 March 2012.

6 Ethnic Chinese entrepreneurship in Penang

Over the years, policies, strategies, initiatives and incentives to promote SME development have been charted in all of Malaysia's economic development plans. According to the SME Annual Report 2011, there are 645,136 SMEs in Malaysia in 2010 up from 552,804 in 2003, which accounted for about 97.3 per cent of total business establishments. They employ 56 per cent of the total workforce and account for 19 per cent of the total exports of the country. Of these 645,136 SMEs, 90 per cent are in the service sector, 5.9 per cent are in manufacturing and 1 per cent are in the agricultural sector (Table 6.1). Out of the total SMEs, almost 80 per cent are micro enterprises with the majority of those in the service sector.

The data from the tables[1] show that the share, or perhaps more correctly the contribution of SMEs to GDP, has increased from 28.5 per cent in 2001 to 31.2 per cent in 2009. The two key value-added contributors are the service and manufacturing sectors (Table 6.2). Though a large majority of business establishments in the country are SMEs, their contribution to the GDP still leaves much room for improvement.

Malaysian SMEs, in terms of contribution to GDP, lag behind, compared against their counterparts in developed economies as well as some of the neighbouring countries (Figure 6.1).

Table 6.3 shows that the state of Selangor led in total number of SMEs with about 99,000 or 18 per cent of the entire surveyed enterprises reported in the 2005 census. This was followed by Kuala Lumpur (17.7 per cent) and Johor (10.3 per cent). While the number of SME establishments of micro enterprises (73,273 or 16.8 per cent) and medium enterprises (2,854 or 22.4 per cent) in Selangor exceeded other states, Kuala Lumpur has the largest number of small enterprise establishments (33,069 or 32.9 per cent). However, one common characteristic found across all states in Malaysia is that at least 70 per cent of their SMEs are micro businesses, except in the Kuala Lumpur area.

Table 6.1 SMEs by economic sector

Number of establishments	Census of Establishments and Enterprises 2005 (Reference Year 2003)				Economic Census 2011 (Reference Year 2010)			
	Total	SMEs	Percentage of SMEs over total	Percentage of SMEs over total SMEs	Total	SMEs	Percentage of SMEs over total	Percentage of SMEs over total SMEs
Services	477,525	474,706	99.4	88.6	591,883	580,985	98.2	90.0
Manufacturing	40,793	39,373	96.5	7.2	39,669	37,861	95.4	5.9
Agriculture	34,486	34,188	99.1	6.2	8,829	6,708	76.0	1.0
Construction	–	–	–	–	22,140	19,283	87.1	3.0
Mining & Quarrying	–	–	–	–	418	299	71.5	0.1
Total Establishments	552,804	548,267	**99.2**	**100**	662,939	645,136	**97.3**	**100**

Source: Census of Establishments and Enterprises 2005 and Economic Census 2011, Department of Statistics, Malaysia

In 2010, SMEs accounted for **97.3%** from the total of 662,939 establishments compared to **99.2%** in 2003. SMEs' concentration in the services sector increased from 87% previously to 90% or 580,985 establishments. Meanwhile, 6% of total SMEs (37,861) were in the manufacturing sector, followed by 3% in the construction sector (19,283) and the remaining 1% (6,708) in the agriculture sector and 0.1% in the mining and quarrying sector. The significant change is that the share of SMEs in the agriculture sector has declined substantially from 6.2% previously to 1% mainly attributable to exclusion of farmers and smallholders which represent a big community under the agriculture sector.

- In the **services sector**, SMEs are mainly in the **distributive trade sub-sector** (wholesale & retail trade services), including repair of motor vehicles and motorcycles, followed by **food and beverages** services and **transportation** & storages services (refer to Chart 2).

Chart 2: Percentage Share of SMEs in the Services Sector by Sub-sectors

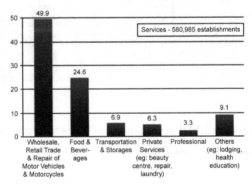

*Note: Others include accommodation, private health care, and education.
Source: Economic Census 2011, Department of Statistics, Malaysia

Table 6.2 Contribution of SMEs to GDP by key economic activity in Malaysia (constant 2000 prices)

Year	2001	2005 % Share to GDP	2009
Agriculture	2.5	2.4	2.4
Mining & quarrying	0.05	0.04	0.04
Construction	0.9	0.8	0.9
Manufacturing	8.5	9.0	8.1
Services	17.4	17.3	20.1
Total value added	28.5	29.0	31.2

Note: Total value added after taking into account undistributed Financial Intermediation Services Indirectly Measured (FISIM) and import duties.

Source: Department of Statistics, Malaysia, 2012.

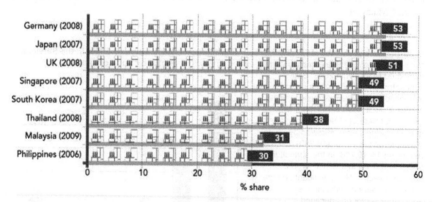

Figure 6.1 SME contributions to GDP in selected countries (% share)

Source: SME Annual Report 2009/10.

6.1 SMEs in Penang

In Penang there were more than 26,000 SMEs in 2005, or nearly 5 per cent of the total SMEs of the nation, as seen in Table 6.4. Of these, 80 per cent were in the micro size category. The remaining was classified as small businesses (17 per cent) and medium-size businesses (3 per cent).

Penang is one of the main manufacturing powerhouses in Malaysia, with many established MNCs and local large companies based in the state. The SMEs form important supply chain arteries in Penang's manufacturing sector. In 2005 there were almost 2,500 SMEs in Penang's manufacturing sector, which made up about 9.2 per cent of the total SMEs in the state (Table 6.5).

Table 6.3 Number and percentage share of SME establishments by state in Malaysia, 2005

State	Micro	% Share	Small	% Share	Medium	% Share	Total SMEs	% Share
Selangor	73,273	16.8	22,396	22.3	2,854	22.4	98,562	18.0
W.P. Kuala Lumpur	60,835	14.0	33,069	32.9	2,914	22.9	96,865	17.7
Johor	45,630	10.5	9,485	9.4	1,356	10.7	56,491	10.3
Perak	37,872	8.7	5,567	5.5	691	5.4	44,144	8.0
Kedah	33,531	7.7	3,066	3.0	432	3.4	37,040	6.8
Kelantan	34,075	7.8	1,528	1.5	198	1.6	35,810	6.5
Sarawak	25,377	5.8	6,601	6.6	1,081	8.5	33,071	6.0
Pahang	24,917	5.7	2,742	2.7	399	3.1	28,066	5.1
Penang	21,422	4.9	4,527	4.5	803	6.3	26,761	4.9
Sabah	18,915	4.3	4,901	4.9	978	7.7	24,803	4.5
Terengganu	22,112	5.1	1,415	1.4	207	1.6	23,740	4.3
Malacca	16,520	3.8	2,696	2.7	407	3.2	19,629	3.6
Negeri Sembilan	14,911	3.4	2,275	2.3	369	2.9	17,561	3.2
Perlis	5,549	1.3	340	0.3	31	0.2	5,922	1.1
Total SMEs	434,939	100.0	100,608	100.0	12,720	100.0	548,467	100.0

Source: Census of Establishments and Enterprises 2005, Department of Statistics, Malaysia.

Table 6.4 Number of SME establishments by sector and size in Penang, 2005

Sector	Micro	Small	Medium	Total SMEs	%
Penang	21,422	4,527	803	26,752	4.9
Other states	413,517	96,081	11,917	521,515	95.1
Total SMEs	434,939	100,608	12,720	548,267	100.0

Source: Census of Establishment and Enterprises, 2005 by Department of Statistics, Malaysia.

Table 6.5 Profile of SMEs by sector and size in Penang, 2005

Sector	Micro	Small	Medium	Total SMEs in Penang	%
Manufacturing	1,205	1,071	180	2,456	9.2
Services	19,161	3,406	607	23,174	86.6
Agriculture	1,056	50	16	1,122	4.2
Total SMEs in Penang	21,422	4,527	803	26,752	100.0

Source: Census of Establishment and Enterprises, 2005 by Department of Statistics, Malaysia.

Table 6.6 Percentage share of SME enterprises by state, 2005

State	Micro	Small	Medium	Total SMEs
Selangor	74.4	22.7	2.9	100.0
W.P. Kuala Lumpur	62.8	34.2	3.0	100.0
Johor	80.8	16.8	2.4	100.0
Perak	85.8	12.6	1.6	100.0
Kedah	90.6	8.3	1.2	100.0
Kelantan	95.2	4.3	0.6	100.0
Sarawak	76.8	20.0	3.3	100.0
Pahang	88.8	9.8	1.4	100.0
Penang	80.1	16.9	3.0	100.0
Sabah	76.3	19.8	3.9	100.0
Terengganu	93.2	6.0	0.9	100.0
Malacca	84.2	13.7	2.1	100.0
Negeri Sembilan	84.9	13.0	2.1	100.0
Perlis	93.7	5.7	0.5	100.0
Total SMEs	79.3	18.4	2.3	100.0

Source: Derived from Census of Establishments and Enterprises 2005, Department of Statistics, Malaysia.

Most of the SMEs, as well as the small and medium industries (SMIs), involved in manufacturing activities are in the subsectors of electrical and electronics, fabricated metal products, plastic products, paper products, machinery and precision tooling, textile and apparel and food processing.

6.2 Ethnic Chinese entrepreneurship in Penang: on SMEs and SMIs

According to Lim and Teoh (2012), it is tricky to define an SME. They cite the United Nations Industrial Development Organisation (UNIDO) for stating that the definition of SMEs is a significant issue for policy development and implementation. Because of this, a clear definition of SMEs in the business context one wants to analyse thus depends primarily on the purpose of the SME in a particular context. Because of this complexity there are various definitions and criteria adopted by different countries to define SMEs. Some refer to the number of employees as their key criterion, others use invested capital; others use a combination of number of employees, invested capital, sales and industry type. Malaysia has adopted a definition of SMEs to facilitate identification of SMEs in the various sectors and subsectors. An enterprise is considered an SME in each of the respective sectors based on the number of full-time employees or annual turnover (Lim and Teoh 2012: 36–37).[2] Small and medium enterprises in the manufacturing, manufacturing-related services and agro-based industries are enterprises with full-time employees not exceeding 150 or with annual sales turnover not exceeding RM

25 million. Small and medium enterprises in the services, primary agriculture and ICT sectors are enterprises with full-time employees not exceeding 50 or with annual sales turnover not exceeding RM 5 million.

To make matters more complicated, there has been some confusion over the difference between SMEs and SMIs. I have often come across an oversimplified use of these terms in speeches by policy makers and even in the academic literature. Chin Yee Whah, from the University Sains Malaysia, defines the difference between the two as follows:

> *Small and medium sized industries (SMI)* refers to enterprises primarily involved in manufacturing of all sectors (such as electrical and electronic products, textile and apparel, steel and basic metal, fabricated metal products, machinery and equipment, non-metallic mineral, food processing, paper and paper products, wood and wood products, rubber-based products, plastics and plastics products, transport equipment, pharmaceutical and professional equipment, etc.). Small and medium sized enterprises *(SME)* refer to a broader group that comprises non-manufacturing industries, mainly in trading (buy and sell only), commerce activities, such as retail organisations in all sectors. In fact, both SMIs and SMEs can become suppliers to public listed companies (PLCs) and MNCs, depending on their products and type of business they are involved in.[3]

A local entrepreneur from Penang, Khoo Cheok Sin,[4] further argues that it is important to distinguish between the two types of companies and thus suggests the following two categories: (1) SMIs that manufacture components and parts, and/or provide manufacturing-related services to the MNCs in Malaysia and overseas; and (2) SMIs that manufacture finished goods for (a) the domestic markets, (b) overseas markets and (c) both domestic and overseas markets.

This distinction is important as each category of SMIs faces different challenges and has different needs. According to Khoo, this will help policy makers to understand each category better, and will go a long way to address their respective needs. SMIs specifically refer to manufacturing companies, not just high-tech companies but also low-tech and labour-intensive industries such as textile industries. If one is only interested in high-tech companies in the manufacturing sector then it is more accurate to use SMI. If one's research also includes ICT, which is also high-tech but classified under the services sector, then SME is more accurate.

The reasons for having chosen to employ the term SME rather than SMI in this study are first, that SMI and SME are used interchangeably in the current literature. Previous literature often used the SMI term. However, as industries developed over time, the services sector also began to expand, thus forcing researchers who study business enterprises to amalgamate the manufacturing and service enterprises as SMEs to avoid conceptual confusion. The second reason for using the term SME in this study is that SMIs in Malaysia are mostly owned by the ethnic Chinese and to avoid the NEP regulations, many ethnic Chinese have established a number of companies in the names of family members and relatives. Often more than one company is registered under the same business address. For example, company A is in manufacturing and company B is in marketing but both are owned by the same persons. Thus, to stay under the NEP radar, ethnic Chinese-owned SMEs set up holding companies. Because of this practice, it is, when studying ethnic Chinese businesses, less appropriate to use the term SMI, as it only includes the manufacturing companies and not the service (marketing) companies.

Based on this definition of an SME, a characteristic of the ethnic Chinese SME community in Penang can be summarised as follows: about 90 per cent of the industry in Penang can be classified as SMEs, the majority of which are owned by Malaysian ethnic Chinese. During an interview in August 2007 with representatives from the Chinese Chamber of Commerce in the state capital Georgetown, it was emphasised that the typical ethnic Chinese SME is currently undergoing a change. They are not only family-run enterprises but are evolving into more complex and diversified entities, the specific characteristics of which depend on the size and constitution of the individual company. The micro or 'mom and pop' ethnic Chinese SMEs are typically very small family-owned and -run companies that produce a narrow range of products. This is especially the case if they are suppliers to major local or foreign companies. The most efficient have hired professional, not necessarily ethnic Chinese, managers to run the business in an 'arm's length' mode, but maintain control over the business strategies themselves. Interestingly, the development of such strategies is based on generally acknowledged ethnic Chinese modes of networking. For example, *guanxi* ways of networking constitute an important strategy, thus matching the general stereotype of ethnic Chinese business practices (Mak and Kung 1999; Cribb 2000; Jakobsen 2007).

It is thus possible to divide the Penang ethnic Chinese SME community into three main categories: first, a 'classical' one consisting of wholly-owned and managed SMEs (mainly micro SMEs); second, wholly-owned SMEs that are more or less run by a professional (that is, not family) management according to 'arm's length' principles but make use of 'classical' ethnic Chinese business strategies and network practices (mainly small and some medium SMEs), and finally, those SMEs that are about 50 per cent or less owned by ethnic Chinese entrepreneurs, are professionally managed and combine 'classical' ethnic Chinese strategies and network practices with modern market-seeking techniques, pushing them towards the upper level of the SME category and perhaps into the category of public listed companies (PLC), thus leaving the SME category altogether.

6.3   The relationship between SMEs and PLCs

In discussing the relationship between SMEs and PLCs in Penang, the CEOs of PLCs such as Pentamaster and Perusahaan Sindi SDN informed me that they were not that keen on working with MNCs, as there was no real research and development (R&D) spin-off in this kind of collaboration. The MNCs were more focused on production, not an exchange of R&D with the PLCs. This indicates that there exists an asymmetrical relationship between MNCs and PLCs. To further explore this, I interviewed a local entrepreneur who knows this issue quite well.[5]

According to this informant, it is important to classify PLCs according to the nature of their business: (1) contract manufacturing for MNCs, (2) provider of ancillary services to MNCs, and (3) manufacturer of industrial and consumer products for domestic and overseas markets. The first two categories are dependent on the MNCs to further development of their business. The so-called transfer of technology that these two categories feed on consists of outsourcing parts of the MNC production operations that require lower levels of technology, are labour intensive and require a rather low level of professional skills. Basically, these firms are the workhorses for the MNCs. There have been cases of MNCs motivating a numbers of PLCs to compete in bidding for the MNCs' products and services for the barest profit margin to survive in the race just to get the orders. Inevitably, those companies that lose out in this competition become insolvent and are foreclosed by the banks. There are, of course, some success stories but these are either being progressively eroded by competitors from Vietnam, China and India, or the companies become so dependent on the MNCs for orders that they have to close down if the MNCs choose to move their production lines to more cost-effective countries.

There are two main reasons behind this differentiation of the Penang SME community. First and foremost, there is an ever entrenching global market economy that forces structural as well as organisational changes on the companies to establish arms-length notions of ownership and management, and to venture outside the immediate domestic market to expand their reach. I shall deal with this subject in more detail in Chapter 7. The second reason for this differentiation is the notion of a special mind-set on behalf of the ethnic Chinese entrepreneurs, and how it manifests itself in an open market economy like the Malaysian one. This is a hugely debated subject that even blends into a discussion of class relations in Malaysian society.

For example, Khoo Boo Teik[6] warned against putting too much emphasis on ethnicity although it is important to have a firm grip on it when discussing the political economy of Malaysia. Class aspects also need to be taken into account, as they run across ethnic borders. There is an intriguing relationship between class and ethnic linkages. The higher up in the class system an entrepreneur is, the less ethnic linkages have an effect on business relations. Here Malay, Indian and ethnic Chinese businesspeople mingle freely among each other, together with the political establishment, forming an oligarchy that has its own agenda for how to develop itself and Malaysia. This is also a development that can be observed in Penang. At the bottom of this system, that is, where the power distance to the top is at its greatest, one finds the small companies and the so-called little people, who have no or very little access to financial resources and political influence. Here perceptions of class are replaced with a gradual hardening of ethnic and religious boundaries, which makes cross-cultural interaction difficult. At this level, the three main ethnic groups do not mingle unless they are forced to do so, either professionally or when entering public spaces.

Zooming further in on this level the following shows, according to Khoo Boo Teik, how divided the three ethnic groups are in relation to each other. The Malays generally live outside of Georgetown in the villages, taking care of their own businesses, especially in agriculture and minor restaurants/food stalls, encapsulated as it is in Islam. The Hindus are mainly living in the poor areas, especially of Georgetown, taking up employment as construction workers or working in comparable categories if not working in the service and retail sectors (sometimes owned by ethnic Chinese). They too are attending to religious activities as a normal part of everyday life. The ethnic Chinese own about 90 per cent of all SMEs within retail, wholesale, restaurants and all sorts of minor production companies. The majority practise their Buddhist and/or Taoist faith that guides them through most aspects of life. They live in Georgetown and in every other small and medium town in Penang. For these three ethnic groups, access to political power varies considerably. However, as they constitute the main part of the population in Penang, they enjoy great attention from the power holders, especially at election time.

The groups in between these top and bottom societal levels are capable of merging class relations and ethnic grievances in order to be heard politically. Interestingly, Khoo stressed that class matters are suppressed by the authorities, as they, according to them, are potentially dangerous for political stability. For example, any initiative to organise labour unions is not popular with the authorities, who look upon such activities with great suspicion. This is why grievances from this level of the population have their roots in class matters but are nonetheless channelled through ethnic grievances.

This also explains why political parties in Penang, and in Malaysia in general, are not based on class but on ethnicity. The relationship between ethnicity and class, as Khoo suggests, is thus shaped like an hourglass, with the opposite blend of ethnic and class relation at each end: at the upper end class relations prevail, which in practical terms means a collusion between economic and political power, and in the lower end ethnic linkages prevail, which in practical terms means that society is divided along ethnically defined class fault-lines. In between these extremes one has the middle class that manipulates the relationship between ethnicity and class relations. For example, Malay SMEs are weak in terms of economics but strong because of their relationship to the political establishment, which is mainly controlled by the *bumiputra*. Ethnic Chinese SMEs are strong because of their firm grip on the economy but weak because of a lack of relations to the political establishment controlled by the *bumiputra*.

In sum, class issues are definitely also on the agenda here but they take on a different form compared to, say, Europe. One has to look further into the complex field of ethnicity to see how class issues are channelled through ethnic grievances. For example, Pentamaster is an interesting case here, as the executive chairman maintained that because of the affirmative action policy, Malaysia is not utilising its capabilities to the fullest because of the brain and capital drain. Developing further on this line of argument, several other CEOs from ethnic-Chinese-owned companies said that top-level non-Malay workers as well as top non-Malay intellectuals are leaving Malaysia because of the affirmative action policy that exercises ethnic discrimination thus reinforcing the brain drain. The only solution to this problem for companies, be they SMEs or PLCs, is to go global to grow and develop further. I shall discuss this in more detail in Chapter 7.

6.4 Exploring the mind-set of ethnic Chinese entrepreneurs

To further explore the position of the ethnic Chinese in Malaysia, this time from an ethnic perspective, and relate that to their strong position within the economy, are we then to accept the definition of the ethnic Chinese entrepreneur as provided by former Prime Minister Mahathir? Mahathir claimed that the Malays do not match the aggressiveness of the ethnic Chinese, a minority group accustomed to fighting for their existence because of their precarious social position. What are the drivers behind Mahathir's proposition that the ethnic Chinese have developed a mind-set of entrepreneurship and robustness that has carried them forward to the present dominant economic position in Malaysia? And finally, if ethnic Chinese entrepreneurs really are that aggressive and innovative, why is Malaysia still caught in the middle income trap?

It is possible to distil three main explanations or versions behind what drives the ethnic Chinese entrepreneurs in a multi-ethnic Malaysian policy context. First, according to informants, the mind-set that governs the majority of the ethnic Chinese SMEs originates from the fact that most of them are family owned and managed, which in many cases results in an inclination to show off personal success rather than reinvesting profits in new technology, know-how and management systems. In other words, they are not interested in an expansion of their companies, but prefer to spend whatever economic spin-off to enjoy life.[7]

The second version is based on the idea that the ethnic Chinese mind-set is mainly governed by the *bumiputra* policy. This alludes to the fact that even though ethnic Chinese entrepreneurs would like to obtain government contracts, Malay entrepreneurs and government-linked companies (GLCs) are generally allotted the most lucrative and biggest contracts. The consequences of this racially informed policy are that the ethnic Chinese then send their children to other countries, together with the advice that they should not return to Malaysia, because they will have a difficult time getting good salaried jobs, as the latter already are more or less earmarked for *bumiputras*. This perception is also behind those ethnic Chinese businesspeople who move their businesses out of Malaysia as well as those academics who take up positions outside Malaysia.[8] The key words here are then 'brain drain' and 'capital drain' due to a perceived difficulty in progressing and expanding, academically as well as business-wise in Malaysia.

The third version is critical of the two other versions, stating that they are based on superficial observations. According to informants, they represent an oversimplification. Experience has shown that behind any successful SME there are one or more entrepreneurs, who can identify business opportunities, mobilise necessary resources, take risks and expand vigorously in a focused manner, thus earning a satisfactory reward in terms of profit. Successful enterprises therefore could not be realised from people with the aforementioned negative mind-set.

The ethnic Chinese SMEs in particular are motivated by profit and self-interest, just like entrepreneurs of any other ethnic group, including their Western counterparts. If growing their business by applying improved technology and better management systems can increase the profitability of their enterprises, they will do this after due diligence to assess the probable value-added outcomes of such initiatives. It is therefore imperative to probe more deeply into the underlying factors to understand how such impressions of a negative mind-set of ethnic Chinese entrepreneurs comes about.

According to a local entrepreneur, his contact with and observation of ethnic Chinese SMEs points to the following two set of factors to explain the above: First, conditioned by three generations as migrants and later as naturalised citizens, the ethnic Chinese overseas (*huaqiao*) had generally adopted a low public profile mind-set in the host country, in this case Malaysia, due to various kinds of politically inspired and ethnically motivated preferential treatment schemes. It is thus natural for the ethnic Chinese to demonstrate overt reluctance to disclosing what, how, when and why they embark on upgrading their business and management systems. Self-interest and personal protection dictate the need to navigate cautiously along a given growth trajectory covertly to avoid the official radar screen – a direct consequence of prevailing inter-ethnic mistrust and suspicion, often a result of undue interference from public officials and politicians. Second, ethnic Chinese SMEs generally exercise financial prudence in managing their businesses. Where long-term business interests require the use of better technology, they would employ only cost-effective technology appropriate for that purpose. There exists a general aversion to unproven 'state-of-the-art' technology that involves initial high capital outlay. According to informants, some ethnic Chinese entrepreneurs have had bad experiences with some MNCs that have outsourced specific manufacturing operations to them on the condition that these ethnic Chinese entrepreneurs invest in new technology including machinery, equipment and operating systems. Lured by the promise of future orders based on outsourced components and products, which can amount to hundreds of millions of dollars, these ethnic Chinese entrepreneurs invest heavily by reducing earnings and obtaining expensive bank loans in relation to the project, only to find out that the promised orders did not materialise. These companies became insolvent and had to close down. It is therefore common to find the ethnic Chinese SMEs only sourcing for appropriate technology at international trade exhibitions or engaging their in-house technical expertise and/or trusted consultants in engineering to improve their already existing manufacturing hardware and software. In the aforementioned cases, they maintain strict secrecy about such initiatives. This explains why visitors to the factories of ethnic Chinese SMEs are kept away from the technology-sensitive operation areas.[9]

Having outlined the three main perceptions of the ethnic Chinese entrepreneurial mind-set, the next step is to investigate what types of companies relate to which of the three perceptions. The first version, according to interviews, characterises representatives from the governmental economic facilitators such as investPenang that works mainly to attract major SMEs, PLCs and MNCs to increase the level of

FDI inflow in Penang. The ethnic Chinese SMEs referred to as being not interested in upgrading their companies are generally those companies that are not capable of attracting FDI themselves, as they are mainly working within service and small-scale production for the domestic market. These companies are thus side-tracked in the official schemes for further industrialisation of Penang.

The second version is forwarded by representatives from the non-governmental economic facilitators such as Penang Skills Development Centre (PSDC) that among other things works to upgrade the ethnic Chinese SME environment as well as the SMEs themselves, thus taking over where official organisations have lost interest. This is, however, not an easy task as many of these companies feel left out of the overall industrialisation process and have therefore retired into a position of disillusioned self-gratification. These perceptions are reinforced by a perception of racial discrimination on behalf of the ethnic Chinese, thus leaving no room for further improvement unless the affirmative action policy is abolished.

The third version of the ethnic Chinese mind-set comes from those individuals who still believe in the overall industrialisation schemes even though there is room for improvement, not only with reference to an abolition of the affirmative action policy, but also because of the diligence and inventiveness of the ethnic Chinese themselves. For several generations the ethnic Chinese have weathered all sorts of problems and difficulties, so why should they not be able to withstand and thus overcome this challenge? This position is taken by those sections of the ethnic Chinese SME community that still feel that their importance as the economic backbone of the overall industrial environment will someday be recognised by the powers that be and thus integrated into the overall industrialisation process as equal partners in relation to all the other companies in this process regardless of ethnic origin.

To further illustrate this complexity three case studies of SMEs are presented in the following chapter. The main focus here is partly to show how to navigate this highly politicised inter-ethnic environment as an entrepreneur and partly to illustrate the mind-set that drives the way the entrepreneurs manoeuvre this complex socio-economic field.

Notes

1 The data on SMEs in Malaysia and in Penang are taken from *Penang Monthly*, issue 2.12, February 2012.
2 The following is based on definitions provided by 'Small and Medium Industries Development Corporation' (www.smidec.gov.my/index.jsp). For further information on the SME community in Penang, see *Penang Economic Monthly*, 9(4), April 2007, and *Penang Monthly*, 2(12), 2012.
3 Chin Yee Whah, personal communication, March 2008.
4 Khoo Cheok Sin, personal communication, March 2008.
5 Because of his request, I am not naming this contact. Personal communication, March 2008.
6 The following is based on an interview with Khoo Boo Teik, University Sains Malaysia, March 2008.

7 Because of the sensitivity of the subject, the informants from several different SMEs have been made anonymous. All data in this connection were collected during interviews with informants on the basis of personal communication, March 2010.
8 It is interesting to note that about one-third of the staff at ISEAS in Singapore is Malaysian ethnic Chinese.
9 Personal observations and communication with ethnic Chinese entrepreneurs, March 2008.

7 Navigating the socio-economic landscape in Penang

Three case studies

The notion of glocalisation and the consequences of societal embeddedness on the economy have been discussed in Chapters 1 and 3, followed by a discussion in Chapter 6 of the mind-set this has produced among ethnic Chinese entrepreneurs. The following three case studies from the SME community in Penang have been chosen to show how the global and the domestic economy impact each other as well as to show how the complexities of various societal factors influence the functioning of the economy. The first two cases represent SMEs that match the definition of an SME in a Malaysian context provided in the previous chapter. The last case represents what the owner has defined as a big medium-sized enterprise (BME) that is listed on the Malaysian stock exchange. The three companies are CKS Engineering Sdn. Bhd, RC Precision Engineering Sdn. Bhd. and Pentamaster Corporation Bhd. They are organised into a discussion of company history, ownership structures, network practices, market and company relations and finally relations to public and non-public economic facilitators.

7.1 CKS Engineering Sdn. Bhd.

7.1.1 Company history

CKS Engineering Sdn. Bhd.[1] was established in 1997 and today has about fifty employees. CKS specialises in providing customised, knowledgeable solutions in precision sheet metal fabrication. The company offers integrated services that include design, manufacturing and after-sales support to both MNC and local customers in telecommunications, power technologies, electrical and electronic, construction and consumer industries. Serving a variety of customers and industries since its establishment, CKS is constantly scanning the market for new developments and has dynamically adapted the necessary changes in equipping its facilities with the latest machinery, developing its employees to deliver customised solutions and customising its processes and services to meet customer needs.

It is a family-owned company started by three family members back in 1997. Later one of them, the current managing director, Mr Tan Teong Sit, bought the other two out and thus became the sole owner. He is married to Ms Kok Kar Fong, who is the managing director of the company. He works on getting new customers and she manages the production floor.

7.1.2   *Ownership structure*

This is a typical ethnic Chinese family-owned company. They previously had a branch outlet before consolidating into the current premises. They have not reached a stage yet of setting up related sister companies, thereby becoming a holding company, like many other ethnic Chinese-owned SMEs. In terms of ownership and management of the company, it now consists only of family members. The employees are more ethnically diverse. They mainly come from south India, Nepal and Bangladesh, together with a few Malays on the production floor. The main problem in this connection is when the workers' working permits expire or when they leave the company for other reasons, then the company owners have to employ new workers, training them from scratch. This creates some problems in relation to the workflow in the company.

In terms of upgrading the workforce, the company is constantly sending its workers to courses organised by outside agencies, especially the PSDC. The workforce is divided into an A team and a B team, which alternate in terms of attending training programmes. This means that when team A goes on an upgrading course then team B continues working in the company and vice versa. The managers upgrade their qualifications mainly based on experience and through interactions with their partners. Ms Kok is very insistent on teamwork. It is a kind of mantra in terms of how this company is managed. Everyone in the company participates in various teams, thus integrating the different sectors of the company. A Confucian mode of organising the company as described in several books on Chinese company organisation was not on the agenda here (Dirlik 1996; Redding 1996; Gomez and Hsiao 2001). When specialists among the staff invent new ways of optimising work processes or new products they present their ideas to their respective teams, and if accepted by them the ideas are taken to the management and discussed in detail. If accepted at this level, they are implemented accordingly. According to Ms Kok, 'we in the management do not know exactly what is going on in the different production phases. The workers do and they know best. We are all here to learn from those who know best. This is how this company works'.

Upgrading the workforce this way is quite interesting. It does not follow a master plan but depends on what kind of new challenges they are facing when signing contracts with buyers. The background for this strategy is thus governed by customisation processes of the products the customers want and can thus be defined as being carried out in an ad hoc manner, seeking maximum flexibility in this connection. Furthermore, in this way they do not just upgrade technologically for the sake of upgrading but always in relation to the specific challenges that competition in the market demands as well as through the customisation process. A Chinese saying in this context could well be, 'crossing the river by feeling the stones'.

For now the family can still handle the management of the company, but they are contemplating buying professional management expertise to further optimise the workflow in and the outward reach of the company. If the company continues to grow as it is currently doing, then a professional management team might become necessary to manage the growth of the company. Ms Kok is very aware of this. In relation to opening the company up for foreign investors, this is, according to her, not yet necessary, but again, if the company is to grow further, then that would be necessary. As for now they are only producing for the domestic market but they are planning to begin exporting their products. Actually, they have already filed the necessary papers for doing just that but have not yet received a reply from the authorities.

7.1.3 Network practices and relations to domestic and global markets

As mentioned earlier, the management team consists of family members whereas the workforce is multi-ethnic. In relation to the latter, there is no preference for employees from any specific ethnic background. Contacts are exclusively made on the basis of qualifications, which are most profitable for the company.

Looking ahead, CKS would still be concentrating mainly on the domestic market but has planned to enter the export market in a small way as a kind of test. However, this initiative is still on the drawing board and no specific strategies have been formulated in this connection. In case they take up exporting, however, they are aware of the dangers of only connecting to MNCs, as the latter might move to another market in Southeast Asia if that suits their needs better. And in this case, subcontractors and suppliers have only two choices: either to follow the MNCs they are connected to or stop operating as a company, as the latter's production capabilities would be exclusively linked to servicing that particular MNC. The CKS management has discussed the possibility of joining an alliance with similar companies but has only just started this discussion. When asked whether the global market forces them to think globally, they say yes. As the domestic market is becoming more competitive, in part because of greater integration into the global market and in part because of more competition from foreign companies, it forces CKS to be more focused on upgrading, not only the management and workforce, but also the machinery and technology that they currently employ in the various production processes.

When discussing their access to funding at, for example, the Bank Perusahaan Kecil & Sederhana Malaysia Berhad, also referred to as the SME bank, to ensure further expansion and/or upgrading technology, the managers say that it is not possible for them to get another loan from the SME bank. They thus have to find funds from elsewhere in order to grow their company. According to them, the SME bank seems to favour *bumiputra* entrepreneurs over other ethnic entrepreneurs. The reason for this apparent customer differentiation might originate from the fact that the bank is owned by the federal government and as such is following the affirmative action policy as formulated in the NEP that originated in 1971. One of the requirements pertaining to this policy is to promote the active participation of *bumiputra* in business by providing them with relatively easy access to loans. As a consequence of this policy, about 80 per cent of the customers in the commercial banks in Penang are ethnic Chinese businesspeople, whereas *bumiputra* entrepreneurs only constitute a fraction of these banks' customer base, according to informants. These banks know that the ethnic Chinese businesspeople almost always paid their loans back while several *bumiputra* entrepreneurs were not able to do that because of a relatively high rate of business failures.[2]

Ms Kok also thought of other ways of raising capital, for example in the form of venture capital. This is somewhat more problematic as it means the family would lose control over the company during a five-year period, as a venture capitalist would take over the company during this period to secure their investment. To my surprise, she did not see this as a problem. If they could get more capital to expand and the cost of doing so was to reduce their level of ownership for a certain period of time, this was acceptable to them. The most important thing was that the company could continue to grow. I suspect the reason behind this acceptance was the same as in the case of employing professional management and allowing foreign investors to enter the company, namely that if CKS is to survive over time, such input of capital and new management systems is necessary.

Another important question was whether the company felt that the government's economic development plans have benefitted the SME sector and in particular the sector that this company represents. They are of the opinion that both the previous and the present state governments are bypassing certain sectors of the SME community. It is difficult to obtain loans and the government is more interested in those companies that are servicing the MNCs, as the latter are important for the government in terms of attracting FDI.

In relation to whether the so-called SMART Centre initiative from investPenang[3] is having an impact on this company, Ms Kok says that they are not familiar with the initiative and furthermore that they do not have any relations with investPenang. CKS is thus on its own, concentrating on doing business and not signing up for governmental initiatives to help SMEs move up the value chain. They are not even in contact with the Chinese Chamber of Commerce so as to have an organisation to follow up on their needs. Paul Ang, the chairman for the South-West Chamber of Commerce in Penang, has several times tried to get this company to sign up for his chamber of commerce, but they keep saying, '*next time we will sign up*'. So far nothing has happened.

7.2   RC Precision Engineering Sdn. Bhd.

7.2.1   Company history

RC Precision Engineering Sdn. Bhd. (RC) was founded by four engineers who were previously employed at different MNCs.[4] RC began operating in 1993 and in 1998 the company had two employees. In 2003 it had 35, in 2006, 120, in 2009, 150, and in 2012 it had 168 employees. All of them are trained to handle various technical requirements for RC's international customers. RC started out as a small-scale producer of machine parts as well as being an equipment service provider to local companies in Penang. Over the past two decades, RC has progressed to serve companies worldwide, using its technological prowess in fabrication, machine assembly, design development and subcontract manufacturing to provide quality-driven engineering solutions to original equipment manufacturers (OEM) of various kinds of machines worldwide. RC was certified as ISO 9001:2008 in August 2009 by SIRA Certification Service UK.

Furthermore, RC is capable of strengthening partnerships with OEM customers by being their appointed technical representative and value-adding services sector and spare parts manager. By having a local representative close to the customer, RC is capable of supporting OEM customers such as Pentamaster Corporation Berhad in Penang, to stay ahead of global competition and eventually penetrate new markets in Asia. RC also caters for other local companies such as the previous LKT Industrial Berhad, bought by the Singaporean investment house Temasek Holdings in 2008, and several other listed and non-listed companies.[5] RC assigns technical teams for specific customers to handle project management, turnkey projects and transfer of technology. Finally, RC has a close working relationship with a sister company in Bologna, Italy.

7.2.2   Ownership structure

This company has never been a family-owned company. The owners come from all three main ethnic groups in Malaysia and the company is thus not confined to a specific ethnic group, as about 90 per cent of other SMEs in Penang are. The core group in this company is bound together by various types of qualifications rather than ethnic linkages.

For management and staff upgrading as well as team-building procedures, the company has a specific budget. There is a great emphasis on creating a loyal mind-set towards the company. Several outings with staff and management take place during the year. The staff is furthermore entitled to various kinds of incentives and saving schemes for the benefit of the employees to boost loyalty towards the company and probably also as a way of keeping them from moving on to a competitor. In relation to upgrading of technical staff, the managing director, Mr Ravichandran, told me that they practise in-house staff training. The senior staff trains the junior staff. The basic idea behind this is that every employee in the technical sector should be able to not only construct and service the various machines for the customers, but should also be responsible for putting together a work team to build the machines. Finally, the individual employee is expected to be able to organise the whole value chain when creating the machines, identifying pertinent suppliers and acting as consultants in relation to customers, as well as organising after-sales service.

In other words, when Mr Ravichandran lands an order for a specific type of machine from a customer he has met at a trade fair, he immediately contacts one of his senior staff and asks this employee to initiate the more detailed aspects of constructing the machines directly with the customer. This employee thus has full responsibility for seeing this particular order through. This way of dealing with customers gives RC maximum flexibility in relation to changing market demands and conditions.[6] The organisational structure of RC can thus be identified as being flat and not hierarchical as otherwise maintained by so-called specialists in Asian company structures (Gesteland 2005) or organised along Confucian-like lines, as argued by Hofstede (1984).

7.2.3   Network practices and relations to domestic and global markets

This company is indeed a multicultural company. There is a Chinese house temple on the first floor and a Hindu god at the entrance. The staff consists of Malays, Indians and Chinese. There is no policy of networking along ethnic lines. Inter-ethnic issues have never been on the agenda in this company. This can be confirmed just by looking at the company composition, both its leadership and staff.

To the question of whether this company is concentrating and directing its efforts towards the domestic market, the answer is, 'definitely not!' They manufacture their products in Penang and then export them to their partners abroad, in particular to Bologna in Italy. In relation to the company's internationalisation strategy, they have employed a multi-pronged approach. They supply public listed companies and MNCs in Penang and similar companies throughout Malaysia, but also venture abroad on the basis of personal networks, the use of middlemen and participation in trade fairs, and so forth. Mr Ravichandran does the actual internationalisation of RC. He travels to trade fairs in France, the United States, Canada, China, Japan, Vietnam and the Philippines to present RC's products and services. As this internationalisation strategy is dependent on one person's sales efficiency on the international market, it makes the overall internationalisation process fairly vulnerable. As a new development in this connection, European companies are beginning to contact RC through their Web page, thus making the company less dependent on the outcome of personalised business links and travels.

The global market forces RC to think globally. As the US and European markets have still not recovered after the current economic crisis, RC is beginning to look to Asian markets, especially in China and India. Whether this is where their major markets will be depends on what happens in the United States and Europe. The global market has always had a big impact on the way RC operates. Even though this is a company that has dealt with the global market from its inception, it is not what can be called 'born global', as it also caters to the domestic market.

7.2.4   Relations to public and non-public economic facilitators

RC has an interest in investPenang's economic development plans, but so far has not really benefitted from this connection. For example, the SMART initiative started by investPenang in January 2010 has had no impact on RC, as RC does not use the kind of services that investPenang provides. Instead, RC has chosen to engage the Malaysian Investment Development Authority (MIDA) and the Malaysia External Trade Development Corporation (MATRADE), as RC not only caters to the domestic market but, increasingly, the global one. Disregarding investPenang as an economic facilitator in relation to both the local and global markets, RC has instead chosen to engage the Penang Automation Cluster (PAC), which acts as an effective pressure group on the Penang state government and its various industrial policies. RC felt that investPenang did not get enough funding from the post-2008 Penang government to carry its various initiatives through. However, this was not to be seen as a critique of the current state government, but rather as an indirect critique of the federal government, as the latter provides the Penang state government with a smaller overall grant as a way of punishing Penang for turning towards the opposition after the national election in March 2008.

Finally, RC does not have contact with any of the chambers of commerce in Penang because of the multicultural composition of staff and management, as all the chambers of commerce in Penang are divided along ethnic lines except for the South-West Chamber of Commerce mentioned earlier that is based on a multicultural platform. RC feels it is duly represented through its links to the PAC.

7.3   Pentamaster Corporation Bhd.

7.3.1   Company history

Pentamaster was established in 1991 and is today a leading company providing advanced manufacturing automation solutions and services to help worldwide customers meet their productivity challenges and maintain the edge required for success in the ever-competitive global business environment.[7] Through its six subsidiaries it provides an integrated range of services in technological solutions, manufacturing of automated and semi-automated machinery and equipment, designing and manufacturing of precision machinery components, as well as design, assembly and installation of computerised automation systems and equipment. Its core competencies include: mechanical engineering design, software programming technology, control engineering and technology, imaging vision technology and electronic and instrumentation design. Pentamaster's technologies and solutions can be deployed across a host of industries worldwide, ranging from semiconductor, computer, automotive, pharmaceutical, medical devices, electrical and electronics, food and beverage and consumer products to general manufacturing. Pentamaster had an annual turnover of about US$ 20 million in 2011 and has 250 employees.

Discussions with the executive chairman, Mr Chuah Choon Bin, took place at Pentamaster in Mr Chuah's office in the main industrial hub in Penang Bayan Lepas. He is not the stereotypical ethnic Chinese businessman but rather an internationalised entrepreneur who regards the global economy as his main market, as the local market is not yet ready for his high-end product portfolio. He himself had designed the factory as well as the headquarters in which we had our meetings. It is not organised along *Feng Shui* lines, as he does not believe in this philosophy. Rather, he designed it according to his own liking and not towards some specific Chinese prescriptions. In a sense he is representative of the new generation of ethnic Chinese business leaders, who are pragmatic about culture and business practices. In the words of Nisbeth *et al.* (2001) and Gesteland (2005), for example, he is a deal-oriented rather than a relational-oriented businessman. As such, he does not fit into the stereotypes of Asian entrepreneurs as otherwise described by the two authors.

Mr Chuah sees Pentamaster as neither an MNC (even though it has representatives and sales offices in the United States, Ireland, Germany, Italy, India, Thailand, Indonesia and Singapore), a conglomerate (even though the company has six subsidiaries) nor an SME (as it is far too big to fit into this category). Instead, he defines it as a listed BME that consists of six subsidiaries[8] organised in the form of a holding company, which he heads.

7.3.2   Ownership structure

Mr Chuah owns 40 per cent of the company and is also the executive chairman. Even though he said that it is not a family-dominated company in the typical ethnic Chinese sense, his brother-in-law, Mr Tan Boon Teik, was the chief executive officer. However, none of the subsidiaries was headed by a family member but by carefully selected professionals.[9] When asked about the nature of his company, he stresses that it is an ethnic Chinese company and that most of the employees in the subsidiaries are ethnic Chinese. Pentamaster is not managed according to stereotypical ethnic Chinese business practices. It moves and develops according to the changing tides of the global market to stay in business.

He is not interested in increasing the size of the company, because, he said, smaller companies are more flexible and adaptable to changing business conditions. In discussing ownership and management, he mentions that there are *bumiputra* on the board of directors, but they are non-independent non-executive officers, meaning that they do not manage or run the company. Furthermore, despite the fact that Pentamaster has *bumiputra* on the board, Pentamaster is not a government-linked company. After listing, a company like Pentamaster would no longer need to have *bumiputra* directors on its board.

Pentamaster is not engaged in the Penang SME environment, as it finds the technological know-how and managerial skills too low in this segment of the local industry. Furthermore, SMEs in Penang seem reluctant to upgrade their companies in terms of technology and knowledge to move up the value chain. Pentamaster has its own R&D section, thus moving the company continuously up the value chain, which is necessary to survive in the global market. According to Mr Chuah, the Penang SME community is very Chinese in the sense that they are almost all family owned, and managed accordingly. They are weakly organised amongst themselves, making them disadvantaged relative to their global competitors. Despite these differences between Pentamaster and the SME community, a representative from the Chinese Chamber of Commerce told me on another occasion that Pentamaster is used as a role model for SMEs to follow.

7.3.3 *Network practices and relations to domestic and global markets*

The Penang SME community is vulnerable when facing and engaging global competition. Interestingly, it seems as if it does not help that most of them are members of the Chinese Chamber of Commerce. This is because the SMEs are organised along classical ethnic Chinese company modes, as discussed earlier. In general, major companies like Pentamaster do not relate to the chambers of commerce, as they are in a different category of industries than those the chamber generally caters for. Companies like Pentamaster are more internationally oriented whereas the companies that the Chamber of Commerce encompasses and nurtures are more service-oriented towards the domestic market. According to Mr Chuah, the current SME community is also weak because the Penang state government does not take SMEs seriously, that is, nurture them in such a way that they become an economic asset in the way the Singaporean government has done (Ng 2002). Mr Chuah suggests that the Penang state government should urge people to buy products from the SMEs to boost their production levels as well as encouraging them to upgrade in terms of technology and management practices. Otherwise they have no future in a globalised economy.[10]

Turning to corporate culture, we discussed how MNCs have dealt with the schism of maintaining the headquarters and subsidiaries as a coherent unit and at the same time allowing individual subsidiaries to deal with the opportunities and constraints emanating from the host market, thus creating a potential conflict between headquarters and subsidiary (Kostova and Roth 2002). Mr Chuah said that the core elements in what he has defined as Pentamaster corporate culture are adaptability and flexibility. The company has a rather flat organisational structure, as that is necessary to deal with the volatile nature of the global market. In this respect, Pentamaster is definitely not managed along Confucian modes, as otherwise suggested by Gesteland (2005).

In relation to the MNC environment in Penang, he was not really following this, as his company has its own R&D section and several sales offices and representatives around the world. Another and perhaps more important reason is that the kinds of products that Pentamaster produces are not compatible with the kind of products the MNCs were concentrating on. Pentamaster specialises in automation, whereas the MNCs in Penang were geared towards high-tech manufacturing.

Probing further into why Pentamaster is not collaborating more with the MNCs to take advantage of the potential spill-over effects, he replies that the MNCs are only interested in a company's products, R&D and local know-how. In most cases there are no spill-overs. They keep their R&D as well as intellectual property rights (IPR) for themselves. Because of this, he does not relate to the MNCs. As such, they are not good for the local economy, as they do not necessarily benefit the public listed companies and/or the SME community. They are basically minding their own business and do not care about the ramifications of their presence in the host economy. The politicians in the Penang state government have not understood this. They focus intensively on the MNCs, as the latter for them represented an important inflow of FDI, which the government needs in order to implement its various development plans. Mr Chuah confirmed my suspicion that the government neglected the non-FDI-producing segment of the SME community and concentrated instead on those SMEs and public listed companies that by themselves or together with the MNCs brought in the much-wanted FDI.

Instead of focusing on the MNCs, Mr Chuah focuses on companies of similar size as his own and exchanges both R&D and IPR with them, but only those that operate in the United States, the EU and certain parts of Asia. He has a factory in China, but he would never exchange such sensitive information with his ethnic Chinese partners, as he believes that would turn them into his competitors. This appears to be the essence of his internationalisation strategy, that is, to internationalise cautiously, step by step, so as not to lose control over the company's core competencies or the IPR to his products to partners and/or potential competitors.

In discussing the actual internationalisation process, I asked him how Pentamaster approached a foreign market. It was first and foremost through personal connections and participation in fairs. Even though fairs are not that effective, one does meet other similar companies and get to know people who one might want to link up to later on. Another way to internationalise is to go through investPenang and/or MIDA. These economic facilitators have the expertise to advertise his company abroad but unfortunately it does not bring that many new customers to Pentamaster. A final mode to internationalise is to hire consultants to work out specific internationalisation strategies for Pentamaster, but this is a very expensive solution. As he formulated it, 'we Chinese are rather stingy when it comes to use money on that kind of activity. There must be other ways to go about approaching new markets'. The most effective mode of internationalising, according to Mr Chuah, was to engage in business alliances with pertinent companies, as that would definitely be both a cost-benefit approach and a more productive way of entering a foreign market.

Again, according to Mr Chuah, in a new trend in international business that he was rather keen on, European companies are looking up Asian companies on the Internet to suggest and initiate collaboration. This is something that he expected he could benefit from in the future. He did not describe whether he himself would make contact with pertinent European companies in this manner. For now he would stick to already established modes of contacting potential customers and clients through participation in international fairs and through investPenang, and more importantly, through MIDA and MATRADE. Commenting further on investPenang, he notes that it can only promote or facilitate different kinds of foreign and local industry matches but not close a deal. Only MIDA can do that. A consequence of this is that every foreign investment, in the form of FDI or foreign-local business deals, has to be approved by MIDA. This constitutes a federal bureaucratic bottleneck when making business deals that could otherwise have been dealt with locally.

Mr Chuah then elaborated on his business strategies when entering a foreign market. He has a very ethnic Chinese way of relating to customers, both domestic and internationally. The basic ingredient is first and foremost trust. He is of the opinion that legally enforced contracts have a tendency to increase transaction cost and foster bureaucracy. For him, empathy between business partners is much more important. Furthermore, he does not employ economic models when working out new strategies but relies instead on past experience. A second very important element in his strategies is the reputation of his company. When people recommend it to others or it is discussed, for example, by me in my academic works, then potential customers become aware of Pentamaster. He has the same pragmatic approach towards his competitors. He is not afraid of them, even though they compete against each other, as they collaborate on other issues, for example in the form of business alliances when entering new markets. He thus relates to his competitors on the basis of co-opetition, which fits perfectly into the third main aspect of his internationalisation strategy, that of alliance making.

Returning to the way Pentamaster is internationalised, marketing abroad and manufacturing at home also constitute an upper limit on Pentamaster's internationalisation process, as this combination might constitute a problem for a further internationalisation due to increasing transaction costs in relation to delivering products to foreign customers. He was keenly aware of this but has not yet found a solution to this. He wants to expand further abroad but is unsure of how to approach this, now that an upper limit has already been reached. He could hire consultants, but that is forbiddingly expensive and Pentamaster is too small a company to provide him with a kind of in-house think tank on how to internationalise further. He is interested in how the Danish windmill giant Vestas is currently changing its internationalisation strategy, that is, building production sites close to the market to minimise transportation costs, but this was something he will work on in the near future. The only thing he is sure of is that a new strategy has to be based on a flexible approach. This is the only way of moving around in a volatile market, both domestically and internationally.

7.4 Innovation and entrepreneurship: how to get out of the middle income trap

During an interview with Mr Ravichandran from RC Precision Engineering, he argued that there is a dual economy in Malaysia, a private one and one that consists of government-linked companies (GLC). If one ventures from the private sector to the GLC sector because of an interest in government contracts, then one should be prepared to get involved with Malay businessmen, who might have a different mind-set on how to do business. I was informed by another informant that even though Malay businessmen went bankrupt, this was not the same as saying that they went out of business. They still had access to government funding and contracts because they were Malays. Furthermore, one has to be prepared to hand over 30 per cent equity to a Malay (sleeping) partner, or if you were lucky, a real Malay entrepreneur. This is a federal government requirement for contracts involving government projects.[11]

As Mr Ravichandra was not interested in having a Malay (sleeping) partner even though it might make him a wealthy man, this made him on par with Mr Chuah, as both RC Precision Engineering and Pentamaster are operating in the private sector of the Malaysian economy. As such, Mr Ravichandra was on his own when doing business, which is also why he is so heavily engaged with business partners abroad, again like Pentamaster. The question now is whether this dual structuring of the Malaysian economy impacts industrial innovation and whether the Malaysian economy can avoid the clutches of the middle income trap that so many people engaged in business development in Penang and beyond are currently discussing.

As Chan Huan Chiang from the Penang Institute pointed out, there is a rather large pool of talent in Penang so this is not the reason for the current lack of innovation in industry, thereby keeping Penang in the middle income trap. Mr Ravichandra attributes this situation to three other factors. The first is the government's heavy focus on attracting FDI, thus making it the main driver of the economy in Penang. According to Mr Chuah, this in itself does not foster innovation because of the fact that technology and management transfer from MNCs to the subcontracting SMEs is of little value when talking about increasing the level of innovation in the local business environment. The second factor is the dominance of low-level manufacturing within the high-tech industry. For now, this sector absorbed most of the local workforce and now has to rely on foreign workers because of a full employment situation. This means that companies have to fight hard to maintain their most qualified workers to prevent 'job-hopping', which again has led to increasing wage levels. However, this does not lead to more innovative modes of upgrading local businesses, which leads us back to what Chan was saying, that there is currently *a lack of incentive to innovate* as entrepreneurs are not forced by a lack of labour to develop new products or introduce new automated manufacturing systems thereby indirectly maintaining the economy in the middle income trap.

Are SMEs capable of contributing to new levels of innovation? A representative from investPenang said that there was the capacity to do so, but not the mind-set. The current situation of full employment has also had an impact, as it does not create a need to innovate. People were satisfied with what they got, thus buying bigger houses or bigger cars instead. This was something that investPenang was working on, trying to explain to the SMEs that if Penang and Malaysia wanted to move up the global value chain, they had to become more innovative and risk minded. Otherwise other markets in Southeast Asia would become more attractive to foreign investors and local SMEs would lose out in terms of potential growth opportunities.

The third factor for a lack of innovativeness is the current level of brain drain in Penang as well as more generally in Malaysia. According to a 2011 World Bank report on brain drain in Malaysia, it is important to relate the notion of brain drain to the notion of diaspora. According to the report, the Malaysian diaspora is large and expanding. Actually the diaspora has grown rapidly, almost quadrupling over the past three decades. The report estimates that in 2010 the diaspora constituted about one million people. The diaspora is geographically concentrated and ethnically biased. Singapore alone absorbs 57 per cent of the total diaspora, with most of the remainder residing in Australia, Brunei, the United Kingdom and the United States. Ethnic Chinese account for almost 90 per cent of the Malaysian diaspora in Singapore. They are equally overrepresented in the OECD countries. About a third of all Malaysian migration is related to intellectual brain drain. Malaysia's rate of brain drain is somewhat skewed in terms of occupation. The skilled diaspora is now three times larger than two decades ago. Malaysia's brain drain is thus concentrated on a narrow skill base. One out of ten Malaysians with a tertiary degree migrated in 2000 to an OECD country. This is twice the world average; including migration to Singapore makes this two out of ten.[12]

Why this increase in the Malaysian diaspora and why this close connection to intellectual brain drain, especially in Penang? One of the reasons is the federal government's affirmative action policy that favours Malays over ethnic Chinese and Indians. Another reason is 'butterfly-picking' of the best students from, for example, University Sains Malaysia (USM) and other institutions of higher learning in Penang by foreign companies, especially Singaporean ones. This leaves only the second-best students for the domestic market, creating a situation in which the industry cannot get the skilled labour it needs to expand and develop.

During an interview with Ms Loo Lee Lian, the head of investPenang, in March 2011, she said that investPenang was working hard to turn that situation around. When asked what kind of relationship investPenang had with, for example, USM, she said unfortunately they did not have that many contacts with USM academics, but that they were always open to new collaboration. According to one of my colleagues from USM, Chin Yee Whah, USM and investPenang did not work that much together. This fits well with what Mr Yoon Chon Leong from BizWise Consulting informed me about during a course on global management in Penang in March 2011. He stated that the capabilities that USM has in relation to high-end industrial development were way behind the needs of the industry. That was the main reason why there were only few working relationships between investPenang and the university.

Returning to the interview with Ms Loo, she then moved on to a discussion of the middle income trap. She was aware of the problems that this generated. This problem was very real because of the political focus on FDI instead of a more concerted effort to focus on innovation to push Penang further up the value chain. An important aspect in this connection was again the brain drain and the Malaysian diaspora of professionals, who did not return to help Penang in its drive to redesign the industrial environment towards more innovation-driven initiatives. According to Ms Loo, investPenang was working on it, especially in relation to the Malaysian diaspora in Singapore that was made up of 'butterfly picked' entrepreneurs and top students from Malaysia, including Penang, that the affirmative action programme had alienated and thus motivated to migrate. Many of those have set up their own companies in Singapore. Because of the sunk costs involved in this connection they were not interested in moving their companies to Penang. Thus, investPenang is trying to get them to invest in Penang, indirectly improving the innovation process and thereby lifting Penang out of the middle income trap.

Concerning innovation, Mr Chuah from Pentamaster said that what also blocked the innovative environment in Penang were the Confucian-like relationships between those in power or those having the means to finance innovation, and those who have the ideas but not the means. That in itself was a hindrance as innovation, according to him, thrives best in a more flat or democratic environment. Mr Chuah continued by saying that it is important to define what is meant by innovation when discussing this concept. He then rhetorically asked whether innovation was when you make an existing product more efficient or fine-tune it, or whether it is when you develop a new product that does not already exist on the market. He preferred the latter definition. Here he referred to Schumpeter (1934), who distinguished between *invention* as an idea made manifest, and *innovation* as an idea applied successfully in practice. We are thus talking about a new product and not an improvement of an existing product.

During a related discussion, Mr Ravichandra observed that innovation does not have to mean either/or. He did not believe in such a sharp distinction in the definition of the concept. He introduced the concept of 'local innovation' as a mode of innovation that exists between an upgrading of existing products and pure innovation of new products. For example, when he received an order for the construction of a new machine, the customer specified what it should look like and what it should be able to do. The new machine was thus a further development of an existing one that the customer already had. During the actual (re-)construction of the existing machine, the engineers had to invent completely new components for it, otherwise it would not function according to the new requirements. In a sense, this machine represents a combination of fine-tuning and further development of an existing machine and newly designed and thus innovative components, making the machine capable of doing something that it was not capable of doing before. Mr Ravichandra speculated whether this notion of 'partial innovation' represented the final step towards the classical definition of innovation as identified earlier. If this was the case, then the automation industry in the upper end of this sector was already contributing to lifting Penang up the value chain.

Finally, Mr Chuah was of the same opinion as Mr Chan from Penang Institute concerning innovation in Penang, namely that there are many talented and innovative people in Penang so the problem was not one of shortage of people capable of being innovative. On the contrary, the problem was that the practice of innovation was blocked by complacency of the current entrepreneurs. Because it is so expensive to develop and design new products, complacency took over, thus prompting a focus on refinements of already existing products, pushing innovative initiatives into the background.

He then moved on to discuss the relationship between innovation and the middle income trap. Besides the aforementioned problems concerning innovation, there are three other important factors that have to be in place if innovative ideas and new products are to become real. First, the industrial logistics or infrastructure must be of a very good standard. Penang definitely has that. Second, there has to be political stability in order to attract investors who would be willing to support the realisation of innovative ideas and products. Penang has that to a certain extent, perhaps not in relation to the GLC sector, but more in relation to the private sector, as it is here that you find the most innovative and motivated entrepreneurs. Third, there must be a stable and highly educated and well-trained workforce. As this is currently not the case, as discussed in the previous chapter, this is where the real problems arise in Penang and in Malaysia in general, causing one of the main drivers behind the current brain drain. According to Mr Chuah, this is serious. A solution has to be found or investors will shy away from Penang and Malaysia in general and go elsewhere in Southeast Asia and beyond in their search for innovative entrepreneurs to get a positive return on their investment.[13]

There is actually a fourth factor, namely the current emphasis on the importance of the value chain. Mr Chuah was rather critical of the way investPenang was working. He was particularly critical of its focus on FDI, as that did not lead towards what Penang needed the most, namely innovative ideas and products. Being dependent on MNCs for knowledge sharing and technology transfer does not lead to innovation, only further refinement of existing products, as discussed earlier. He felt that investPenang's main idea behind the SME village in Batu Kawan, where the so-called SMART initiative are located, and where various electrical and electronic clusters are to attract and service MNCs when building up their value chain in a Penang cum Malaysian context, was an old-fashioned way of thinking. He said, with the Internet dominating industrial development in many ways, companies like Pentamaster sourced what they needed directly from different suppliers. Not all of them are in Penang, in Malaysia, or even in Asia. Pentamaster is sourcing globally and is thus not dependent on, for example, pertinent SME clusters in this respect.

Because of this mode of sourcing, Pentamaster's value chain is not a closed one but open and thus flexible enough to engage suppliers around the world, thereby not tied down to a certain region or type of market. On this basis, it could be argued that a value chain cannot only be perceived as a tunnel-like construction, but just as much as an octopus-like entity that is constantly moving its arms in all directions in a constant search for suppliers and subcontractors.

This development has not yet dawned on investPenang or many of the other industry facilitators set up by the Penang state government. They still think of the traditional perception of value chain as the only way of managing a company's internationalisation process. A search for suppliers is thus not only not tied to actual markets or regions but is increasingly done in cyberspace. There is a problem here, however. Mr Chuah did not elaborate on it, but if you source globally, on a virtual ticket, you must deal with the actual logistics of sourcing globally, that is, how to move products from supplier to buyer. It seems as if this constitutes the Achilles heel of virtual sourcing.

Notes

1 This company was first visited in March 2010: www.cks-eng.com/.
2 Personal communication, March 2009.
3 The Small and Medium Enterprises Market Advisory Resource & Training Centre (SMART) is an initiative of the Penang state government through investPenang to provide market intelligence, business advice, information and resources and training service to

SMEs in Penang. For more details see www.investpenang.gov.my/smedir/intro.php. Accessed 9 August 2012.

4   This company was visited for the first time in March 2010.
5   For more details see the company Web site www.rcprecision.com.my/.
6   Mr Ravichandran, personal communication, March 2012.
7   This discussion of Pentamaster covers conversations with the executive chairman, Mr Chuah Choon Bin, over a period from July 2007 to March 2011. The Web site to Pentamaster is: www.Pentamaster.com.my/.
8   Pentamaster Technology, Pentamaster Engineering, Pentamaster Solution, Pentamaster Equipment Manufacturing, Pentamaster Instrumentation, Pentamaster Information Technology.
9   Pentamaster annual report 2010.
10   See also *The Star*'s business section on SMEs, 25 June 2007, concerning this issue.
11   Anonymous informant, personal communication, March 2011.
12   Malaysia Economic Monitor: Brain Drain. April 2011. The World Bank, p. 12.
13   Malaysia is already losing inward FDI compared to other Southeast Asian nations such as Indonesia and the Philippines. See for example www.rappler.com/business/20893-philippines-the-new-indonesia. Accessed 10 February 2013.

Part IV

The glocalisation of context

Some concluding remarks

8 On constructing an etic and emic approach when employing international business theories on ethnic Chinese business practices

As discussed in Chapter 4, contrary to the popular idea that the ethnic Chinese of Southeast Asian descent form part of a coherent diasporic ethnic group based on common perceptions of Chinese-ness, this book argues that the ethnic Chinese of Southeast Asian descent consist of several different more or less societally integrated groups, some of which might be linked to a given Chinese-orientated diaspora. This differentiation reflects a variety of impacts originating from colonialism, early nation building and contemporary processes of social and political engineering, when developing a potent national political ideology-cum-national identity. An instructive example of a less positive consequence of such developments is that ethnic Chinese in Malaysia have been subjected to various forms of 'othering' as a direct result of the affirmative action policies initiated in 1971 and still in effect in 2014. Basically, such policies have ascribed the Malaysian Chinese as well as Malaysian Indian communities residing in Malaysia as constituting distinct immigrant minorities, thus making the Malaysian Malay communities an indigenous ethnic majority in the process. As also discussed in Chapter 4, processes of 'othering' have their roots in notions of 'Chinese capitalism'. The latter was defined as constituting a flow of ethnicised capital governed by Chinese kinship and language associations framed in Confucian dogmas (Yao 2002a). The main *modus operandi* controlling this flow is ascribed to *guanxi* affiliations based on *xinyong* or trust.

This book takes a critical stand towards such notions. It has been argued that ethnic Chinese business practices do not typify a specific type of Chinese economy paralleling an open market economy, thus emphasising and employing an approach to the market economy that de-essentialises conceptions of 'Chinese capitalism'. Chapter 6 in particular discussed how the ethnic Chinese business environment in Penang cannot be defined in terms of intra-ethnic relations when it comes to networking and internationalisation strategies, thus deconstructing such preconceptions.

Furthermore, confining a study of ethnic Chinese and ethnic Chinese entrepreneurship to intra-ethnic (business) relations within a given Southeast Asian community gives a one-dimensional perspective of the ethnic Chinese business community. Chapters 6 and 7 in particular discussed how Malaysian Chinese entrepreneurs constitute an integrated part of the Penang and Malaysian business communities and how they relate to the global economy, as well as underlining the importance of recognising that they, too, are deeply integrated into the overall Malaysian institutional environment.

To assess how ethnic Chinese switch back and forth between the national and international realms, Chapter 4 and to a certain extent Chapter 7 discussed processes of diasporisation and de-diasporisation. Riggs' (2001) notion of 'de-diasporisation' in Chapter 4 was especially of interest as it alluded to being localised without becoming absorbed by the local. This means that ethnic Chinese are not sojourners between, for example, China and Malaysia, but citizens of Malaysia. Sociopolitical developments influence whether ethnic Chinese stay in Penang or join the Malaysian diaspora in, for example, Singapore or Australia. I argue that specific sociopolitical developments in a given Southeast Asian nation have to be taken into account when trying to understand those processes that activate or de-activate relations to a possible ethnically related transnational community.

Because of the complexity of how Chinese-ness is socially constructed or deconstructed to accommodate the national vision of '1Malaysia' as discussed in Chapter 3, it is very difficult to generalise about ethnic Chinese entrepreneurs in Malaysia. Even though there might be strong relations between ethnic Chinese entrepreneurs, it is not the same as saying that they relate to each other because of the fact that they share the same ethnic background, regardless of whether we talk about locally or globally oriented Chinese. What we do see is that national political schemes like the Malaysian affirmative action policy make Chinese feel like a coherent ethnic group. On the basis of this, it is possible to hypothesise that ethnic groups and ethnically linked (business) networks, when they are formed, are externally not internally constructed. That is, they are artefacts of forces from the outside, not love from the inside. Thus, ethnic networks are born out of distrust rather than trust. To go a step further, it is possible to argue that networks are formed by ethnic Chinese (businessmen) from a position of weakness, not strength. Taking such a position is to refer directly to the affirmative action policies, which lead to certain levels of societal alienation by the ethnic Chinese. In light of this, (business) networks can be conceptualised as a group strategy – not to build trust per se, but to cope with distrust (Yao 2002b).

When discussing this issue with ethnic Chinese entrepreneurs in Penang, they maintain that it is not ethnicity that is the defining factor when identifying business partners. As they see it, it is what kind of opportunities other businessmen, regardless of ethnic background, can provide. This should deal the final blow to that part of the international discourse on ethnic Chinese business practices that identifies them as being part and parcel of ethnically dominated types of networks, described in the business literature as tribe-like or constituting bamboo networks or underground empires, based on diasporic linkages that, according to Fukuyama (1995), Redding (1996) and Ong and Nonini (1997), typify Chinese business activities and practices.

Stereotypical perceptions of Chinese entrepreneurs do not work when relating actual Chinese business practices to a given societal context, in this case the Malaysian one, because of the dynamic between the global and the local. As stated in Chapter 3, we are looking at a triangular relationship between global business practices, the Malaysian national business context and the societal context in which the two other points in the triangle are embedded. It is the processes between the different points in the triangle that determine the relationships between them. I will discuss this in greater detail a bit later. For now, I will give a more detailed focus on this triangle and how to define the processual aspect of it.

The following discussion of the implications of employing the notion of glocalisation is thus based on inclusiveness, or to use another term, to employ a holistic approach to analysing the triangle. I do recognise that there are three other modes of thinking about the global economy, namely decoupling, spiky or flat, or a qualitative market differentiation. However, according to my perception, these other modes of perceiving the global economy only address two of the corners in the suggested triangle, namely the global political and economic developments and the role of the state, whereas the developments within the civil society are left out of the equation.

In Chapter 3 the actual application of the analytical triangle on Malaysia was discussed. The triangle itself was defined as consisting of (1) how foreign investors 'read' the Malaysian market, (2) domestic societal factors, and finally (3) the impact of the national economic policy in this context. The main outcome of this discussion was that foreign investors could employ a two-pronged approach in deciding whether to enter a foreign market, first, a firm-specific perspective, that is, the foreign company in question, assessing the key economic figures to see whether the company would benefit by entering that particular market. The second approach was based on what can be termed a more generic reading of the given market to assess whether the institutional arrangement of that market would or could secure a long-term investment. The second perspective is especially important as it would provide the investor with insights into whether the 'sunk costs' in the form of production facilities would pay off in the long run, an insight that was mainly based on the impact of societal factors on economic performance.

The point of applying this triangle to Malaysia was to analyse the Malaysian market from an etic and emic perspective. Taking the etic approach first, such an approach would provide us with a point of departure for analysing this market from a critical perspective. As shown in Chapter 3, the main difference between the previous economic model, the NEP from 1971, and the NEM from 2009, is that the latter takes a liberal approach towards the market to further open it up to foreign as well as domestic investors whereas the former is based on a developmental state policy. In relation to the liberal approach towards the market there is an emphasis on economic growth led by the private sector, localised decision-making and a bias towards technologically capable industries and firms, thus providing a basis to attract more FDI to Malaysia. This deviates from earlier economic development practices, such as the NEP, that were based on centralised strategic planning, state participation in the economy and restrictions on foreign skilled workers. These policies have now been taken out of the political and economic equation with the introduction of the NEM. The recommendations from the 'new approach' in the NEM fit well into the current tendencies in the global economy where trade liberalisation and open markets are the dominant issues on the agenda. Seen from this perspective, the NEM tries to accommodate and thus attract international investors to the Malaysian market.

If we now take a look at the third 'leg' of the triangle, the domestic societal factors, we also see that the NEM tries to accommodate private investment by providing more incentives to engage in domestic economic development schemes, especially for SMEs. There is, however, a problem here. The NEM does not address the fundamental issue of the intricate and rather tense relationship between the three main ethnic groups, the Malays and the ethnic Chinese and Indians. Despite all the neo-liberal rhetoric concerning opening up the market for foreign investors and more support for the SMEs in the domestic industrial landscape, the NEM still contains a clause that, although formulated in a softer manner, maintains the affirmative action policy. This is rather problematic, as about 95 per cent of all SMEs in, for example, Penang are owned by ethnic Chinese. It was furthermore demonstrated that the background for an apparent contradiction between an open market, political rhetoric and the maintenance of the affirmative action policy has its roots in the political restraints on the prime minister's ability to fully implement the NEM, confines that emanated from the BN political establishment.

Most of the data that these observations are based on can be termed etic, that is, data deducted from secondary sources collected at local and international research institutions, academic publications and so forth, as well as through interviews with local business entrepreneurs. This is the normal procedure when employing, for example, North's institutional analysis, especially that part discussing the relationship between formal and informal institutions and in particular the impact that informal institutions have on formal ones in terms of functionality and implementation, thus providing an indication of the current state of the target market.

To move beyond these confines and employ an emic approach, three case studies of SMEs were introduced. To demonstrate the complexity of the relationship between the economic and societal aspects, the three SMEs represented a small SME, a medium-sized one and finally a large SME that was about to move beyond the definition of SME altogether because of the number of employees and annual turnover. Despite these differences, all three companies shared the same societal constraints that had negative impacts on their ability to grow. To account for these constraints, an emic perspective was employed. The focus points in this connection were the ramifications that emanated from inter-ethnic relationships and in particular the affirmative action policy that to a certain extent controls and governs these relationships.

The first set of ramifications consisted of how well the individual company was able to manage and thus navigate the highly politicised inter-ethnic relationship. All three companies were more or less confined in their growth forecasting because of the brain drain and capital drain that have their roots in the affirmative action policy. A consequence of this was an overtime developed ability on behalf of the ethnic Chinese entrepreneurs to creatively navigate the thus politicised socio-economic landscape in order to grow their companies. A second major outcome from the affirmative action policy was the confinement within the middle income trap. The key issue here was especially the brain drain affecting both business and academia. Special attention in this connection should be paid to an increasing capital flight that was mainly motivated by a discriminatory policy towards the ethnic Chinese entrepreneurs. This had a serious impact on the economy per se as well as on a gradual deepening of the middle income trap as they are the main industrialists and entrepreneurs in Penang and Malaysia in general. Both the federal and state governments have initiated policies to lure back the ethnic Chinese entrepreneurs to Penang and Malaysia, but so far without much success. In relation to the brain drain within academia, various foreign companies, especially from Singapore, offer the brightest students further education and jobs in Singapore. The ethnic Chinese reinforce this type of brain drain themselves, as they send their children to the best universities available in, for example, Singapore, Australia, the United States and the EU, an opportunity denied them in Malaysia because of the affirmative action policy.

Identifying the root causes behind the ethnicised sociopolitical streams of development and the problematic development of the industrial setup due to the firm grip of the middle income trap is very difficult to do when employing a generic institutional theoretical approach, an approach that was discussed in detail in Chapter 2. Instead, the analyst has to go beyond the current complex constitution of and impact from the informal institutions on the formal ones to develop an analytical approach that is contextually structured to be capable of identifying those subsocietal developments that produce brain drain and capital drain as well as the negative ramifications of the affirmative action policies. It is thus not enough to rely on an etic data collection approach combined with an analytical approach. The analyst should also focus on how individual ethnic Chinese entrepreneurs navigate the politicised inter-ethnic relationship and how they perceive the way these developments infiltrate and govern notions of entrepreneurship in Penang and in Malaysia in general. Collecting the latter kind of data, that is, emic data, can be quite difficult as informants regard this kind of information as highly sensitive. One way of going about it is to develop a kind of *guanxi* or trust relationship between researcher and informants. Once this is done, a sphere of trust and thus mutual confidentiality is built and data will start flowing. However, this is a long-term project that can easily take several rounds of fieldwork for the researcher to establish. The most important theoretical outcome of this kind of dual research strategy, if successful, is a further development and understanding of the different sociopolitical and economic developments that institutional theory builds on, especially the currently fuzzy understanding of how to identify and handle the various normative as well as sociopolitical constructs that govern the flow of developments within the informal institutional environment.

8.1 Global fragmentation of local markets

Moving back to our foreign investor, or the global point in the triangulation that governs the analysis of the Malaysian socio-economic environment, and connecting this point to the societal point in the triangle and focusing in particular on the industrial landscape, an understanding of the dual nature of the Malaysian business setup can be arrived at. I am in particular referring to the split between privately owned companies and the GLCs and the consequences that this split has for the current state of affairs in the Malaysian economy, namely the middle income trap. To go beyond that, again one has to address the affirmative action policy and especially the 30 per cent equity in companies that is to be transferred to Malays.[1] Companies that are owned by ethnic Chinese and comply with the federal government requirements would be eligible for lucrative government contracts. These companies thus fall under the GLC category. The privately owned companies, those that did not fall under the federal governmental requirement of 30 per cent Malay equity, or were too small in terms of number of employees and annual turnover, could thus be termed SMEs mainly owned by ethnic Chinese. As shown in Chapter 7, the owners of these companies that were on a positive growth trajectory employed a strategy of turning their companies into holding companies to avoid the federal government's requirements.

According to informants, the main reasons for not developing their companies into GLCs were first, that they would like to maintain full control over their companies, and second, because they would like to avoid getting involved in inter-ethnic politicisation of their company and the corrupt practices that might follow in this context.[2] There is, however, also a third reason, namely that much of the technological innovation is carried out in the private sector of the Malaysian economy, especially in ethnic Chinese-owned companies. Because of the discriminatory practices inherent in the affirmative action policy towards ethnic Chinese, pertinent innovation potentials are not realised within the Malaysian economy, but employed in an international business context instead. This has the implication that the Malaysian economy is not moving beyond its current state of an efficiency-driven economy and is thus not capable of moving towards becoming an innovation-driven one that is necessary if the political long-term plan as envisioned in Vision 2020 is to be realised.

The real tragedy behind the current developments within the Malaysian economy is not a lack of capability in terms of innovation, but rather an ethnically politicised economic policy that maintains Malaysia in the middle income trap, thus gradually losing out to the other Southeast Asian economies, currently especially the Philippine and Indonesian economies. A consequence of this almost stagnating economy is that innovation, which is the most important factor behind the development from an efficiency-driven economy towards an innovation-driven economy, is redirected from serving the Malaysian economy towards serving the global economy, as this is where entrepreneurs find the most conducive environment for growing their businesses. The societal factors within the triangular approach to the analysis of the Malaysian economy thus show themselves to have tremendous impact on the growth potential of the national economy as outlined in the NEM.

This state of affairs is also a sign of how the global economy penetrates a local economy. This penetration fragments the local economy because of higher levels of competition between local and global companies as well as between local companies. The NEM provides a direct avenue for international companies to establish themselves in the Malaysian market through its open market approach, thus dragging the national and local economies further into the global market, a development that is reinforced by a developmental policy based on attracting FDI. This approach has a negative effect when trying to promote industrial innovation in a local industrial setting as it pushes local entrepreneurs and their innovative initiatives towards the global economy instead.

Paradoxically, the global economy thus constitutes a kind of safe haven for the most dynamic and innovative part of the private sector of the Malaysian economy, thereby leaving a major part of the GLC-dominated sector of the Malaysian economy less engaged with the global economy because of the close relationship between the top players within the business sector and the political establishment, thus deepening the middle income trap for Malaysia. Besides pulling the national economy in different directions, this dual-like structure of the national economy also means that Malaysia is gradually being left behind other Southeast Asian nations in terms of economic development.

These domestic-initiated problems then spill over into how the national economy relates to the global one. As previously mentioned, Malaysia is gradually becoming less capable of attracting FDI compared to, for example, the Philippines and Indonesia, thereby being less able to fulfil its ambition of becoming a developed nation by 2020. This inter-connectedness between national economic aspirations, the societal context in which it operates and how this complex relationship relates to the global economy actually constitutes the epitome of glocalisation as discussed in Chapter 1. The local and the global are thus intertwined to such an extent that the two cannot be disentangled. This bears witness to the impossibility of being able to decouple a national economy from the global one. It also shows that the global economy only exists when linked to a local context. The global thus does not have an existence as an independent entity somewhere 'out there' hovering about local specificities. It is the mutual interdependence between the two that brings life to both of them.

8.2 Contextual imperatives in relation to IB theories

This discussion of the importance of the local in the global and vice versa, as well as the impossibility of decoupling the local from the global due to a complex entanglement of the two, has important implications for the way IB theories can be employed in a given locality. We are talking about contextual imperatives when employing international business theory. There is a double dimension to the contextual imperatives, a duality that is currently not taken into account in IB theories. Most of these theories do take a given locality into account but that is generally based on an etic approach, for example, Dunning's OLI, Barney's RBV and VRIO, Porter's Five Forces and his Diamond and North and Scott's institutional theory, as well as the various approaches to entry modes, just to mention a variety of the most frequently employed IB approaches.

These approaches and theories look at a pertinent locality from the viewpoint of the theory and not from the locality itself, that is, from a dynamic and complex societal context that on the surface presents itself as a construct that can be analysed from an etic perspective. There are two main reasons for this. The first has to do with the nature of the theories themselves. Several of the theories are composite entities, meaning that they are not constructed on the basis of one approach, but are constructs based on several theoretical inputs, thus making them more of a composite paradigm than a single approach-based theory. Dunning's OLI and institutional theory are good examples here. This criticism can also be directed to Porter's Five Forces and his Diamond as well as Barney's RBV, even though these approaches are not as explicitly constructed on a multiple theoretical base of different theoretical approaches as the OLI and institutional theory.

Second, because of their complexity, these composite paradigms lose their empirical base and become vacuum-like entities that can be employed in any given context and locality. This is exactly their Achilles heel. A given context or locality is turned into a case that can be understood when employing these composite paradigms, thus verifying their explanatory power and thus legitimacy in the process. The societal complexity that makes up 'the cases' is thus downplayed and does not have an impact that questions the explanatory power of the composite paradigms themselves.

One of the main aims of this book is to introduce a bottom-up approach that argues that a societal embedment of a given IB theory, regardless of its nature, has to address this embedment, as the latter has the capability of modifying the explanatory power of the theoretical models employed. The crux of the matter is that a given societal context is not static but highly dynamic and that many of the IB theories employed are not constructed to take this fluidity into account. However, the problems in using IB theories, or any theory for that matter, do not end here. Recognising the importance of societal embeddedness when working with these theories is not enough, as a mere recognition of it is still equivalent to employing an etic approach towards the contextual imperatives.

Arguably, this is thus only one side of the coin. The other side consists of taking an emic approach into account as well. Combining the two approaches is equivalent to a holistic approach that again is equivalent to taking the importance of the local in the global into account, thus employing a glocalised approach in IB studies. For the sake of simplicity I selected institutional theory to move beyond the etic approach generally employed in these studies. I focused in particular on the informal institutions that according to the theory have an impact on the functionality and thus implementation of the formal institutions, especially in an emerging market context. As discussed in Chapter 2, the characterisation of informal institutions is generally weak. There are references to normative, religious and cultural imperatives, and as the individuals who staff the formal institutions are also signatures to these normative, religious and cultural values, they impact the functionality and implementation of the formal institutions. This interactive relationship between the two sets of institutions, however, is as close as we get to what constitutes the essence of informal institutions. This book has tried, through an emic approach, to dig a bit deeper into the mores of informal institutions to investigate the societal forces that govern the different actors there.

The basic premise taken here has been that even though the Malaysian economy can be characterised as being heavily influenced by global economics, it is just as much influenced by developments from within the civil society itself. This was documented in Chapter 5, where it was shown how inter-ethnic relations and policies impact the overall political framework, setting the outer limits for what the prime minister can do in terms of changing the social and economic premises in the political arena. It was also taken up in Chapter 7, where the manoeuvrability of ethnic Chinese entrepreneurs in an inter-ethnic landscape was confined by the affirmative action policies, and how that impacted the way these entrepreneurs could grow their companies and the overall economic performance of the Malaysian economy.

The identification of the processes behind these developments was done on the basis of interviews over several years with entrepreneurs, academics and bureaucrats to get their views and impressions behind these developments. On the basis of these interviews it has been possible to put together an emic perspective of the forces that govern developments within the informal institutions, thus qualifying the etic descriptions of the informal institutions as delineated in Chapter 3. The main theoretical objective of this book has thus been fulfilled, namely to qualify the way we are to deal with the study of the informal institutions, thus making the composite paradigm of institutional theory even more pertinent when applied to a dynamic and constantly changing societal context.

8.3 Integrating the four constituent parts: some concluding remarks

The preceding chapters have been organised into four parts, as can be seen in Figure 8.1.

Each part constitutes a section that provides the reader with a framework that gives the information and data needed for the next part. Part I delineates the overall theoretical perspective employed in this book. It is divided into two main sections. The first one discusses the various ways to 'read' the global economy and arrived at a notion of the global economy as being not only global but also glocal, meaning that it is impossible to disentangle the global from the local. This also laid the foundation for a triangulation approach that constitutes one of the cornerstones in this study, a triangle that consists of the global economy, a national economic context and a societal aspect that in its own way conditions the functionality of the two other points in the triangle because of the notion of embeddedness. The second section takes a more detailed look at the theoretical perspective. It discusses various international business theories and finally zooms in on institutional theory, and especially the part of it that deals with the relationship between formal and informal institutions. Here the informal institutions

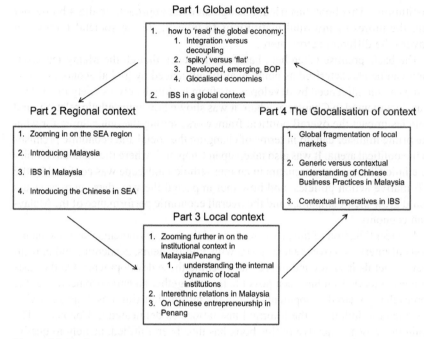

Part 1 Global context

1. how to 'read' the global economy:
   1. Integration versus decoupling
   2. 'spiky' versus 'flat'
   3. Developed, emerging, BOP
   4. Glocalised economies
2. IBS in a global context

Part 2 Regional context

1. Zooming in on the SEA region
2. Introducing Malaysia
3. IBS in Malaysia
4. Introducing the Chinese in SEA

Part 4 The Glocalisation of context

1. Global fragmentation of local markets
2. Generic versus contextual understanding of Chinese Business Practices in Malaysia
3. Contextual imperatives in IBS

Part 3 Local context

1. Zooming further in on the institutional context in Malaysia/Penang
   1. understanding the internal dynamic of local institutions
2. Interethnic relations in Malaysia
3. On Chinese entrepreneurship in Penang

Figure 8.1 Book structure
Source: Own creation. February 2013.

became the ultimate theoretical focus, as I believe it has not been adequately discussed in the IB literature. The main theoretical contribution of this book is thus a qualification of how to analyse the various societal aspects that constitute the different social and political drives within the informal institutional arrangements.

Part II deals with the Southeast Asian regional context. As this book presents a case study on Malaysia, and in particular Penang state, it is important to position Malaysia in a regional context. In order to do that, the Southeast Asian countries of Indonesia, Thailand, Vietnam and Cambodia were selected to help assess the relative political and economic position that Malaysia has in the region. The result of this comparison was that Malaysia is still the top-ranking ASEAN country, although especially Indonesia is rapidly catching up because of very good economic performance combined with a relative easy access to its huge domestic market.

During the analysis of Malaysia in this context, it became clear when employing IB theories, especially the OLI and RBV approaches, that Malaysia is caught in what has been termed the middle income trap, that is, the Malaysian economy is increasingly incapable of maintaining its current regional position because of a lack of national economic development from an efficiency-driven economy towards an innovation-driven economy. One of the main reasons for this is the affirmative action policy that permeates all societal levels, thus bringing to a halt further development of the overall national economy, reinforcing an already serious brain drain and capital drain that is currently crippling the economic and sociopolitical performance.

To go beyond this problematic state of affairs, the focus changed to the main economic agents in the Malaysian economy, namely the ethnic Chinese. Even though they constitute a minority of 26 per cent of the total population according to 2010 figures, they control about 65 per cent of all economic activity in Malaysia. Besides acknowledging this as being the main background for the affirmative action policy, I find it important to understand why the ethnic Chinese take up this position so as to understand the main drivers behind the current ethnic policy in Malaysia.

After having positioned Malaysia in a Southeast Asian context and discussed the internal social, political and economic dynamics of Malaysia, Part III narrowed the focus to the State of Penang. After having outlined the political and economic organisation of Penang, we once again returned to the inter-ethnic relationships in that state, which are quite different from the rest of the Malaysia. Because of colonial factors, the ethnic Chinese have always been the major ethnic group in Penang. During 2009 and 2010 the picture changed and the Malays took over as the majority ethnic group in terms of sheer numbers. In 2011, however, the ethnic Chinese again became the majority ethnic group in Penang, thus underlining the specific ethnic composition in this state compared to the rest of Malaysia. Regardless of whether the ethnic majority situation in Penang has changed in recent years, the political and economic spheres have always been and still are dominated by ethnic Chinese.

To show how ethnic Chinese entrepreneurs navigate the rather heavily politicised inter-ethnic landscape, three SMEs were selected, representing a small, a medium and a 'large' SME/BME to show how the three companies have dealt with the different opportunities and constraints that this landscape confronts them with. The impact on business performance that the affirmative action policy has is striking, especially in terms of funding opportunities or rather the lack of them for ethnic Chinese businessmen and second, the impact of this on industrial innovation. Through interviews, especially with medium and large SMEs, it is clear that the Malaysian economy consists of two more or less interrelated tracks. The first one consists of government-linked companies that, because of their engagements with Malay businessmen, are capable of getting lucrative government contracts. The other track is the private business one dominated by ethnic Chinese entrepreneurs.

The interesting thing to notice here is that it is mainly in this sector that the industrial innovation process takes place. The problem, however, is that this innovation does not benefit the overall Malaysian economy, but in many cases goes directly abroad to business partners in other countries. The consequence of this for the Malaysian economy is a reinforcement and thus a further deepening of the middle income trap for Malaysia. Even though the various government-sponsored economic facilitators did their utmost to lure back the Malaysian businessmen within the Malaysian diaspora, and especially the ethnic Chinese, this is still a work in progress.

The Malaysian economy and society is currently at a crossroads. Should it continue along the lines as outlined in the NEM programme, with continued emphasis on the affirmation action policy, even though it has been renamed 'a market friendly affirmative action policy'? Or, should Malaysia follow the main trends outlined in Vision 2020 in which 1Malaysia is the key word, that is, that every Malaysian regardless of ethnic background has equal access to opportunities offered by the state and economy?

Part IV took its point of departure from Part I. Here the notion of glocalisation was reintroduced as the main argument employed in this book. It would not have been possible to delineate the relationship between the global economy, a national economic context and a societal aspect that in its own way conditions the functionality of the two other points in the triangle, if this approach was not employed in this study. We have seen a very close relationship between ethnic Chinese business practices, inter-ethnic relations and how especially the latter had and still have a major impact on the formulation of national economic developmental schemes, for example, the NEP and the NEM.

The national economic developmental initiatives are thus caught between the ethnic political imperative and the national economic demand for an increased inflow of FDI, a kind of Scylla and Charybdis dilemma as the state has to please both in order to legitimate itself and its policies. This also has an impact on the discussion of whether Malaysia could decouple from the global economy to nurture the domestic economy. By employing the notion of glocalisation, this possibility was rejected because of very close ties between the local and the global. As stated in Chapters 8.1 and 8.2, the global is conditioned by the local context, as the global does not have an existence in itself. Only the local has that and this in a multitude of ways, thus giving both life and substance to the global.

These findings have a big impact on the explanatory power as well as the level of applicability of IB theories on a given locality. As several of the IB theories are developed in almost vacuum-like societal/perfect market conditions, the contextual imperatives, when applied on a local context, have bearing on their explanatory power. This is not to say that IB theories can be discharged; on the contrary, they are still highly pertinent in international business studies. What the present book argues in this context is that IB theories cannot be applied without taking the processes and factors of societal embeddedness into account, and here we are in particular talking about the different social and political drivers within informal institutions. The global market is 'spiky' and contextually conditioned and it is this reality that IB theories have to take into account when being applied. The main contribution of this book is thus that it has tried to give an example of how to deal with the contextual imperative when discussing global economic impacts on a specific locality.

As the attentive reader has probably already observed, the notion of culture has not been dealt with in the last few chapters. Instead the discussion has centred on the manoeuvrability of the ethnic Chinese entrepreneurs in terms of doing business in a politicised inter-ethnic landscape. This narrow focus compared to cultural explanations of ethnic Chinese business practices in a Malaysian/Southeast Asian context has been quite deliberate, as the concept of culture is perhaps one of the most slippery to deal with because of its many different connotations that cover national, organisational and local levels. The relationship between these three and the applicability of culture in general was discussed in detail in Chapter 2. I felt it was necessary to deal with this question, as the use of 'culture' abounds in international business literature, where it confuses more than clarifies as it is so difficult to define. Chapter 2 attempted to clarify why the notion of culture in business studies is problematic and focused instead on what other kind of explanations can be forwarded, thus avoiding the 'veil of mist' in which the use of culture generally clouds business studies.

When dealing with Malaysian social, political and economic matters, this study has avoided employing the notion of culture as an explanatory framework of differences, as such a notion does not explain how these differences came about in the first place, nor does it say anything about the dynamics and drivers behind the relationship between ethnic groups or how that might spill over into the political and economic spheres. When focusing on identifying those dynamics and drivers that are normally identified as 'culturally' constituted, the latter can instead be identified as reflections of those dynamics and drivers, thereby avoiding providing simplified explanations of why the ethnic Chinese, Malays and Indians relate to each other and the society the way they do. This approach, defining culture as a reflection of social dynamics and societal drivers instead of being the explanation itself, is a way of getting deeper into, or perhaps better framed, getting beyond the different elements that populate a generally rather blurred notion of what constitutes informal institutions. Employing cultural explanations of the constituent elements behind informal institutions is actually taking an analytical step backwards and re-introduces stereotypical studies, as those forwarded by Hofstede, Nisbeth and colleagues and Gesteland.

The main argument that this book is based on is, on the contrary, to point towards the importance of being able to identify the different processes that condition the framing of the local contexts. As I have stressed throughout this book, the importance of studying the local through the lenses of a 'glocalised' set of analytical spectacles replaces the notion of cultural explanations that compared to this constitute hindrances for identifying the aforementioned governing societal processes. That is why the notion of culture has been left out of this study. Only by employing a triangular approach to the study of relationships among the global economy, a national economic context and a societal aspect that conditions the functionality of the two other points in the triangle are we capable of excavating the societal processes and drivers that on the surface manifest themselves as cultural iconic representations of what those processes and drivers might look like to the naked eye.

Notes

1 For more details see Chapter 6.
2 According to the Global Corruption Perception Index 2012, Malaysia ranks 54 out of 182 countries.

Bibliography

Ahlstrom, David and Garry D. Bruton (2010) 'International Market Entry', *International Management. Strategy and Culture in the Emerging World.* Cengage Learning.

Amir, Samir (1974) *Accumulation on a World Scale,* Vol. 1. New York: Monthly Review Press.

Anderson, Benedict R. O'G. (1987) 'The State and Minorities in Indonesia', in Cultural Survival Report 22:73–81. *Southeast Asian Tribal Groups and Ethnic Minorities. Prospects for the Eighties and Beyond.* Cambridge: Transcript Printing Company.

Ang, Ien (2001) *On Not Speaking Chinese. Living Between Asia and the West.* London: Routledge.

Appadurai, A. (1991) 'Global Ethnoscapes. Notes and Queries for a Transnational Anthropology', in Richard G. Fox (Ed.), *Recapturing Anthropology. Working in the Present,* pp. 191–210. Santa Fe: School of American Research Press.

Ariffin, Norlela (2011) 'Innovating up to Speed', *Penang Economic Monthly,* 5(May), 8–16.

Banaji, Jairus (1977) 'Modes of Production in a Materialist Conception of History', *Capital & Class,* 3, 1–44.

Barney, J.B. (1991) 'Firm Resources and Sustained Competitive Advantage', *Journal of Management,* 17(1), 99–120.

Barney, J.B. (2001) 'Resource-based Theories of Competitive Advantage: A Ten-year Retrospective on the Resource-based View', *Journal of Management,* 27(6), 643–650.

Barth, Fredrik (1994) 'Enduring and Emerging Issues in the Analysis of Ethnicity', in Hans Vermeulen and Cora Govers (Eds.), *The Anthropology of Ethnicity,* pp. 11–32. The Hague, The Netherlands: Het Spinhuis.

Beh, Loo See (2007) 'Malaysian Chinese Capitalism: Mapping the Bargain of a Developmental State', in Voon Phin Keong (Ed.), *Malaysian Chinese and Nation Building. Before Merdeka and Fifty Years After,* pp. 223–267. Kuala Lumpur: Centre for Malaysian Chinese Studies.

Bolt, P.J. (2000) *China and Southeast Asia's Ethnic Chinese: State and Diaspora in Contemporary Asia,* Westport, CT: Praeger.

Brannen, Mary Yoko (2004) 'When Mickey Loses Face: Recontextualisation, Semantic Fit, and the Semiotic of Foreignness', *Academy of Management Review,* 29(4), 593–616.

Brannen, Mary Yoko (2005) 'What is Culture and Why Does It Matter? Current Conceptualisations of Culture from Anthropology'.

Breckenridge, Carol A., Sheldon Pollock, Homi K. Bhabha and Dipesh Chakrabarty (Eds.), *Cosmopolitanism.* Durham, NC and London: Duke University Press.

Brown, David (1994) *The State and Ethnic Politics in Southeast Asia.* London and New York: Routledge.

Brown, Robin (1995) 'Globalisation and the End of the National Project', in John Macmillan and Andrew Linklater (Eds.), *Boundaries in Question: New Directions in International Relations,* pp. 54–68. London and New York: Pinter Publishers, St. Martin's Press.

Callahan, W.A. (2002) 'Diaspora, Cosmopolitanism and Nationalism: Overseas Chinese and Neo-nationalism in China and Thailand', Hong Kong: City University of Hong Kong, Southeast Asia Research Centre, Working Paper Series no. 35. *Remapping East Asia. The Construction of a Region,* edited T.J. Pempel, pp. 216–235. Ithaca, NY: Cornell University Press.

Carney, M., E. Gedajlovic and X. Yang (2009) 'Varieties of Asian Capitalism: Towards an Institutional Theory of Asian Enterprise', *Asia Pacific Journal of Management,* 26(3), 361–378.

Castles, Stephen and Alastair Davidson (2000) *Citizenship and Migration. Globalisation and the Politics of Belonging.* London: Macmillan Press.

Chen, Ming-Jer (2002) 'Transcending Paradox: The Chinese "Middle Way" Perspective', *Asia Pacific Journal of Management,* 19, 179–199.

Chin, Yee Whah (forthcoming) 'The Future of Small and Medium Sized Enterprises in Malaysia: Constraints and Opportunities', *The Journal of Asia-Pacific Business.*

Chun, Allen (2003) 'Who Wants to be Diasporic?'. Working Paper Series No. 50. Southeast Asia Research Centre. City University of Hong Kong.

Clifford, J. (1994) 'Diasporas', *Cultural Anthropology,* 9(3), 302–338.

Cribb, Robert (2000) 'Political Structures and Chinese Business Connections in the Malay World: A Historical Perspective', in Chan Kwok Bun (Ed.), *Chinese Business Networks. State, Economy and Culture,* pp. 176–192. Singapore: Prentice Hall.

Dirlik, A. (1996) 'Critical Reflections on "Chinese Capitalism" as a Paradigm', in A. Brown (Ed.), *Chinese Business Enterprise,* Vol. I, pp. 17–38. London and New York: Routledge.

Dunning, J.H. (2000) 'The Eclectic Paradigm as an Envelope for Economic and Business Theories of MNE Activities', *IBR,* 12, 141–171.

Dunning, J.H. and S. Lundan (2009) *Multinational Enterprises and the Global Economy.* 2nd ed. Cheltenham: Elgar.

Emmanuel, Arghiri (1972) *Unequal Exchange.* New York: Monthly Review Press.

Evans, P. (2005) 'Between Regionalism and Regionalisation: Policy Networks and the Nascent East Asian Institutional Identity', in T.J. Pempel (Ed.), *Remapping East Asia. The Construction of a Region,* pp. 195–251. Ithaca, NY: Cornell University Press.

Fang, Tony (2006) 'From "Onion" to "Ocean". Paradox and Change in National Cultures', *International Studies of Management and Organisation,* 35(4), 71–90.

Ferguson, Y.H. and R.W. Mansbach (2012) *Globalization: The Return of Borders to a Borderless World?,* London and New York: Taylor & Francis.

Florida, Richard (2005) 'The World is Spiky', *The Atlantic Monthly,* October, 48–51.

Frank, André Gunder (1978) *Dependent Accumulation and Underdevelopment.* London: The Macmillan Press.

Frank, André Gunder and Barry K. Gills (1996) *A Structural Theory of the Five Thousand Year World System.* Available from: www.rrojasdatabank.info/agfrank/structural.html.

Friedman, Jonathan (1998) 'Indigenes, Cosmopolitans and the Discreet Charm of the Bourgeoisie', in Udvalgte oplæg fra årsmøde i 1998. Dansk Ethnografisk Forening, *Grænser for Globalisering,* Aahus and Copenhagen: University of Aahus.

Friedman, Thomas L. (2005) *The World Is Flat: A Brief History of the Twenty-First Century.* New York: Farrar, Straus and Giroux.

Fukuyama, Francis (1995) 'Social Capital and the Global Economy', *Foreign Affairs,* Sep/ Oct. 74(5), 89–103.

Geertz, Clifford (1973) *The Interpretation of Cultures.* New York: Basic Books.

Gesteland, Richard R. (2005) *Cross-Cultural Business Behavior. Negotiating, Selling, Sourcing and Managing Across Cultures.* Copenhagen: Copenhagen Business School Press.

Gomez, Edmond Terence (2004) 'De-Essentialising Capitalism: Chinese Networks and Family Firms in Malaysia', *NIASNytt: Asia Insights,* 3, Sep., 8–10.

Gomez, Edmond Terence and H.M. Hsiao (Eds.) (2001) *Chinese Business in Southeast Asia: Contesting Cultural Explanations, Researching Entrepreneurship.* Richmond, Surrey: Curzon Press.

Granovetter, Mark (1985) 'Economic Action and Social Structure: The Problem of Embeddedness', *American Journal of Sociology,* 91, 481–510.

Guibernau, Maria Montserrat (1996) *Nationalisms: The Nation-state and Nationalism in the Twentieth Century.* Cambridge: Polity Press.

Hall, Peter A. and David W. Soskice (2001) *Varieties of Capitalism: The Institutional Foundations of Comparative Advantage.* Oxford: Oxford University Press.

Hall, Stuart. (1997) 'The Local and the Global: Globalisation and Ethnicity', in Anthony D. King (Ed.), *Culture, Globalisation and the World System. Contemporary Conditions for the Representation of Identity,* pp. 19–40. London: MacMillan Education LTD.

Hannerz, Ulf. (1997) 'Scenarios for Peripheral Cultures', in Anthony D. King (Ed.), *Culture, Globalisation and the World System. Contemporary Conditions for the Representation of Identity,* pp. 122–124. London: MacMillan Education LTD.

Harvey, David (1990) *The Condition of Postmodernity: An Enquiry into the Origins of Cultural Change.* Oxford: Blackwell Publishing Press.

Hofstede, Geert (1984) 'Cultural Dimensions in Management and Planning', *Asia Pacific Journal of Management,* 1(2), 81–99.

Hofstede, Geert (1991) *Cultures and Organizations: 'Software of the Mind'.* New York: McGraw-Hill Book Company.

Holm, Hans-Henrik and Georg Sørensen (1995) *Whose World Order? Uneven Globalisation and the End of the Cold War.* Boulder, CO: Westview Press.

Hutchinson, Francis (2009) *Developmental States and Economic Growth at the Sub-National Level: The Case of Penang.* Singapore: Institute of Southeast Asian Studies.

Jackson, Robert K. (1990) *Quasi-States: Sovereignty, International Relations, and the Third World.* Cambridge: Cambridge University Press.

Jacobsen, Michael (1999) 'Indonesian Nationalism Reconsidered. Scenarios from a Restructuring Society', paper for a workshop on 'Nationalism and Particularism in Present-day Southeast Asia', held at the Royal Institute of Linguistics and Anthropology in Leiden, the Netherlands on 13–16 December, pp. 1–27.

Jacobsen, Michael (2002) 'On the Question of Contemporary Identity in Minahasa, North Sulawesi Province, Indonesia', *Asian Anthropology,* I, 31–58.

Jacobsen, Michael (2004a) 'De-linking the Chinese Diaspora. On Manadonese Chinese Entrepreneurship in North Sulawesi'. Working paper Series No. 60. Southeast Asia Research Centre. City University of Hong Kong.

Jacobsen, Michael (2004b) 'Factionalism and Secession in North Sulawesi Province, Indonesia', *Asian Journal of Political Science,* 12(1), 65–94.

Jakobsen, Michael (2007) 'Re-Conceptualising Notions of Chinese-ness in a Southeast Asian Context. From Diasporic Networking to Grounded Cosmopolitanism', *East Asia: An International Quarterly,* 24(2), June, 213–227.

Jacobsen, Michael and Ole Bruun (2000) *Human Rights and Asian Values: Contesting National Identities and Cultural Representations in Asia.* Richmond: Curzon Press.

Jacobson, David (1998) 'New Border Customs: Migration and the Changing Role of the State', *Journal of International Law and Foreign Affairs,* 443–462.

Jain, Megha, Khalil, Shadab, Le, Angelina Nhat-Hanh Cheng and Julian Ming-Sung (2012) 'The Glocalisation of Channels of Distribution: A Case Study', *Management Decision,* 50(3), 521–538.

Johanson, J. and J.E. Vahlne (2009) 'The Uppsala Internationalisation Process Model Revisited', *Journal of International Business Studies,* 40, 1411–1431.

Kahn, Joel S. (2004) 'Introduction: Identities, Nations and Cosmopolitan Practice', in Joel S. Kahn (Ed.), *Ethnicities, Diasporas and 'Grounded' Cosmopolitanism in Asia,* pp. 2–9. Singapore: Asia Research Institute: Monograph Series, 29 April.

Keesing, Roger M. (1976) *Cultural Anthropology. A Contemporary Perspective.* New York: Holt, Rinehart and Winston, p. 173.

Khanna, T., K.G. Krishna and J. Sinha (2005) 'Strategies that Fit Emerging Markets', *Harvard Business Review,* June, 63–76.

Khoo, Boo Teik (2004) 'Managing Ethnic Relations in Post-crisis Malaysia and Indonesia: Lessons from the New Economic Policy'? In *Identities, Conflicts and Cohesion.* Programme Paper Number 6, August. United Nations Research Institute for Social Development, Geneva, Switzerland.

Kipp, Rita Smith (1993) *Dissociated Identities. Ethnicity, Religion and Class in an Indonesian Society,* Ann Arbor: University of Michigan Press.

Kong, James Chin (2003) 'Multiple Identities among the Returned Overseas Chinese in Hong Kong', in Michael W. Charney, Brenda S.A. Yeoh and Tong Chee Kiong (Eds.), *Chinese Migrants Abroad. Cultural, Educational, and Social Dimensions of the Chinese Diaspora,* pp. 63–82. Singapore, London, Hong Kong: Singapore University Press.

Kostova, Tatiana and Kendall Roth (2002) 'Adoption of an Organizational Practice by Subsidiaries of Multinational Corporations: Institutional and Relational Effects', *The Academy of Management Journal,* 45(1), Feb., 215–233.

Kotkin, J. (1992) *Tribes: How Race, Religion, and Identity Determine Success in the New Global Economy.* New York: Random House.

KPMG, www.kpmg.com/us/en/Pages/default.aspx, accessed 17 March 2012.

Krasner, Stephen D. (1999) *Sovereignty: Organised Hypocrisy.* Princeton, NJ: Princeton University Press.

Krugman, Paul R. and Maurice Obstfeld (2009) *International Economics. Theory and Policy.* 8th ed. Boston, MA: Peason Addison-Wesley.

Li, J. and P.C. Wright (1999) *The Issue of Guanxi: Discrepancies, Reality and Implications.* Hong Kong: Hong Kong Baptist University, School of Business, Business Research Centre.

Lim Wei Seong and Teoh Ai Ping (2012) 'Small and Medium Enterprises – The Drivers of Change', *Penang Monthly,* February, 2(12), 36–40.

Luo Y. (2000) *Guanxi and Business.* Singapore: World Scientific.

Mahathir, Mohamad (2011) 'A Doctor in the House. The Memoirs of Tun Dr. Mahathir Mohamad.' Selangor, Malaysia: MPH Group Publishing Sdn Bhd.

Mak Lau-Fong and Kung I-Chun (1999) 'The Overseas Chinese Network: Forms and Practices in Southeast Asia'. Prosea Occasional Paper No. 26. May.

McKeown, A. (2001) *Chinese Migrant Networks and Cultural Change: Peru, Chicago, Hawaii, 1900–1936*, Chicago, IL: University of Chicago Press.

Nesadureai, H. E. S. (2004) 'Attempting Developmental Regionalism through AFTA: The Domestic Sources of Regional Governance', in K. Jayasuriya (Ed.), *Governing the Asia Pacific*, pp. 37–55. London: Palgrave.

Ng Beoy Kui (2002) 'The Changing Role of Ethnic Chinese SMEs in Economic Restructuring in Singapore: From "Two-legged" Policy to "Three-legged" Strategy', in Leo Suryadinata (Ed.), *Ethnic Chinese in Singapore and Malaysia. A Dialogue between Tradition and Modernity*, pp. 255–275. Singapore: Times Academic Press.

Nisbeth, Richard E., Kaiping Peng, Incheol Choi and Ara Norenzayan (2001) 'Culture and Systems of Thought: Holistic Versus Analytic Cognition', *Psychological Review*, 108(2), 291–310.

North, Douglass C. (1991) 'Institutions', *The Journal of Economic Perspectives*, 5(1), 97–112.

Ohmae, Kenichi (1995) *The End of the Nation State: The Rise of Regional Economies*. New York: Free Press.

Ong, Aihwa (1999) *Flexible Citizenship: The Cultural Logics of Transnationality*. Durham, NC: Duke University Press.

Ong A. and D. M. Nonini (1997) *Ungrounded Empires: The Cultural Politics of Modern Chinese Transnationalism*. New York: Routledge.

Orr, Ryan J. and W. Richard Scott (2008) 'Institutional Exceptions on Global Projects: A Process Model', *Journal of International Business Studies*, 39(4) Institutions and International Business (June 2008), 562–588.

Penang Development News (2003) 'Penang's Industrialisation Journey', pp. 1–24.

Peng, Mike W. (2002) 'Towards an Institution-Based View of Business Strategy', *Asia Pacific Journal of Management*, 19, 251–267.

Peng, Mike W. (2009) 'Leveraging Capabilities Globally', *Global Business*, South-Western Cengage Learning.

Peng, Mike W. and Klaus Meyer (2011) 'Starting International Business', Chapter 11 in *International Business*. South-Western Cengage Learning.

Peng, Mike W. and J. Zhou (2005) 'How Network Strategies and Institutional Transitions Evolve in Asia', *Asia Pacific Journal of Management*, 22, 321–336.

Poh, Heem Heem (2010) 'The New Economic Model – Strategic Policy Directions', *Penang Economic Monthly* (June), 46–49.

Porter, M. E. (1990) 'The Competitive Advantage of Nations', *Harvard Business Review*, March–April, 73–93.

Porter, M. E. (2008) 'The Five Competitive Forces that Shape Strategy', *Harvard Business Review*, January.

Redding, S. G. (1996) 'Weak Organisations and Strong Linkages. Managerial Ideology and Chinese Family Business Networks', in G. G. Hamilton (Ed.), *Asian Business Networks*. Berlin, New York: Walter de Gruyter.

Reid, Anthony (Ed.) (1993) *Southeast Asia in the Early Modern Era: Trade, Power, and Belief*. Ithaca, NY: Cornell University Press.

Riggs, F. W. (2001) *Glocalization, Diaspora and Area Studies*, www2.hawaii.edu/~fredr/glocal.htm, pp. 1–4.

Robertson, Roland (1995) 'Globalisation: Time-Space and Homogeneity-Heterogeneity', in Michael Featherstone, Scott M. Lash and Roland Roberson (Eds.), *Global Modernities*, pp. 25–44. London: Sage.

Ronen, S. 1986. *Comparative and Multinational Management*. New York: Wiley.

Rugman, A. M. and A. Verbeke (2004) 'A Perspective on the Regional and Global Strategies of Multinational Enterprise', *Journal of International Business Studies,* 35, 3–18.

Safran, W. (1991) 'Diaspora in Modern Societies: Myths of Homeland and Return', *Diaspora,* 1(1), 83–93.

Sautman, Barry (2002) *Hong Kong as a Semi-Ethnocracy: 'Race', Migration, and Citizenship in a Globalised Region,* Division of Social Science, Hong Kong University of Science and Technology. Mimeographed Draft of 29 October.

Schein. E. (1985) *Organisational Culture and Leadership.* San Francisco, CA: Jossey-Bass.

Schuilenburg, Marc (2008) 'Citizenship Revisited – Denizens and Margizens', *Peace Review: A Journal of Social Justice,* 20, 358–365.

Schuman, Michael (2010) 'Escaping the Middle Income Trap', *Time: Business and Money,* August 10.

Schumpeter, Joseph A. (1934) 'The Theory of Economic Development', translated by R. Opie from the 2nd German edition [1926]. Cambridge: Harvard University Press.

Scott, W. R. (1995) *Institutions and Organisations,* Thousand Oaks, CA: Sage.

Scott, W. R. (2008) *Institutions and Organisations: Ideas and Interests.* 3rd ed. Thousand Oaks, CA: Sage.

Scott, W. R. (2010) 'Reflections: The Past and Future of Research on Institutions and Institutional Change', *Journal of Change Management,* 10(1), 5–21.

Sheffer, G. (1986) *Modern Diasporas in International Politics.* Sydney: Croom Helm.

Shenkar, O. (2004) 'One More Time: International Business in a Global Economy', *Journal of International Business Studies,* 35, 161–171.

Shuval, Judith (2000) 'Diaspora Migrations: Definitional Ambiguities and a Theoretical Paradigm', *International Migration,* 38(5), 41–55.

Smith, Anthony D. (1990) 'Towards a Global Culture?', in Mike Featherstone (Ed.), *Global Culture: Nationalism, Globalisation and Modernity,* A Theory, Culture and Society, Special Issue, pp. 171–191. London: Sage.

Sperber, Dan and Deirdre Wilson (1986) *Relevance: Communication and Cognition.* Oxford: Blackwell.

Stephenson, Laura B. (2002) 'The Social Democratic Program in LMEs: A Study of Welfare Policy Variation in the Anglo-American Democracies'. Prepared for presentation at the Annual Meeting of the Midwest Political Science Association, Chicago IL, 25–28 April 2002.

Stiglitz, Joseph E. (2006) *Making Globalization Work.* New York: W. W. Norton and Company.

Tan, Chee Beng (1997) 'Comments on "Ethnic Chinese in Southeast Asia: Overseas Chinese, Chinese Overseas or Southeast Asians?"', in Leo Suryadinata (Ed.), *Ethnic Chinese as Southeast Asians,* pp. 25–32. Singapore: Institute of Southeast Asian Studies.

Tan, Mely G. (1997) 'The Ethnic Chinese in Indonesia: Issues of Identity', in Leo Suryadinata (Ed.), *Ethnic Chinese as Southeast Asians,* pp. 33–65. Singapore: Institute of Southeast Asian Studies.

Teo, Peggy (2003) 'The Limits of Imagineering: A Case Study of Penang', *International Journal of Urban and Regional Research,* 27(3), Sep., 545–563.

United Nations Industrial Development Organisation (UNIDO): Industrial Development Report 2009: www.unido.org/fileadmin/user_media/Publications/IDR_2009_print.PDF.

Verdery, Katherine. (1994) 'Ethnicity, Nationalism and State-making', in Hans Vermeulen and Cora Govers (Eds.), *The Anthropology of Ethnicity,* pp. 34–35. The Hague, The Netherlands: Het Spinhuis.

Vertovec, Steven and Robin Cohen (Eds.) (2002) *Conceiving Cosmopolitanism. Theory, Context and Practice.* New York: Oxford University Press.

Wallerstein, Immanuel (1979) *The Capitalist World-Economy.* Cambridge: Cambridge University Press.

Waltz, Kenneth (2008) *Realism and International Politics.* London: Routledge.

Wang, Gungwu (1989) 'The Study of Chinese Identities in Southeast Asia', in Jennifer Wayne and Wang Gungwu (Eds.), *Changing Identities of the Southeast Asian Chinese Since World War II,* pp. 1–21. Hong Kong: Hong Kong University Press.

Wang, Gungwu (1991) 'Among Non-Chinese', *Daedalus,* 20(2), 135–157.

Wee, Vivienne (2004) 'A Cultural Economy of Ethnicity and Capitalism in the Regionalisation of China and Southeast Asia', *NIASNytt: Asia Insights,* 3, Sep., 5–7.

Weidenbaum M. and S. Hughes (1996) *The Bamboo Network. How Expatriate Chinese Entrepreneurs Are Creating a New Economic Superpower in Asia.* London: The Free Press.

Whitley, R. (1998) 'Internationalization and Varieties of Capitalism: The Limited Effects of Cross-national Coordination of Economics Activities on the Nature of Business Systems', *Review of International Political Economy,* 5(3), 445–481.

Wong, J. (1998) *Southeast Asian Ethnic Chinese Investing in China,* USA: Columbia University, East Asian Institute, Working Paper No. 15.

World Bank (2011) *Malaysia Economic Monitor: Brain Drain.* April (61483).

World Economic Forum (2012) 29www3.weforum.org/docs/WEF_GlobalCompetitive nessReport_2012–13.pdf.

Yang, M. M. (1994) *Gifts, Favors, and Banquets: The Art of Social Relationships in China,* Ithaca, NY: Cornell University Press.

Yao, Souchou (2002a) *Confucian Capitalism. Discourse, Practice and the Myth of Chinese Enterprise.* London: RoutledgeCurzon.

Yao, Souchou (2002b) 'Guanxi: Sentiment, Performance and the Trading of Words', in Thomas Menkhoff and Solvay Gerke (Eds.), *Chinese Entrepreneurship and Asian Business Networks,* pp. 233–254. London and New York: Routledge/Curzon.

Yeah, Tricia (2011) 'Reversing the Brain Drain Requires a Paradigm Shift', *Penang Economic Monthly* (June), 40–42.

Yeung, Henry Wai-chung (1998) *Under Siege? Economic Globalisation and Chinese Business in Southeast Asia.* PROSEA Occasional Paper No. 21. June.

Yoshikawa, Muneo Jay (1987) 'The Double-Swing Model of Intercultural Communication between the East and the West', in D. Lawrence Kincaid (Ed.), *Communication Theory: Eastern and Western Perspectives,* New York: Academic Press.

Index

Note: Page numbers with *f* indicate figures; those with *t* indicate tables.

For Product Safety Concerns and Information please contact our
EU representative GPSR@taylorandfrancis.com Taylor & Francis
Verlag GmbH, Kaufingerstraße 24, 80331 München, Germany